Do you love Tunisian Crochet? Then you will love all 15 modern designs in this book. Choose from a hip Poncho, a stylish Boomerang Shawl, a trendy Cowl, a flamboyant Harlequin Scarf, a warm Hat & Mitt Set, or a comfy Jacket to dress up your wardrobe. Add a touch of panache to your décor with a modern Wall Hanging, a terrific Table Runner, a fantastic Floor Pillow, an intriguing Throw Pillow, a cozy Mitered Squares Throw, or chic Placemats. There is also a perfect Storage Basket or a delightful Tote. So, get ready to create all these great designs!

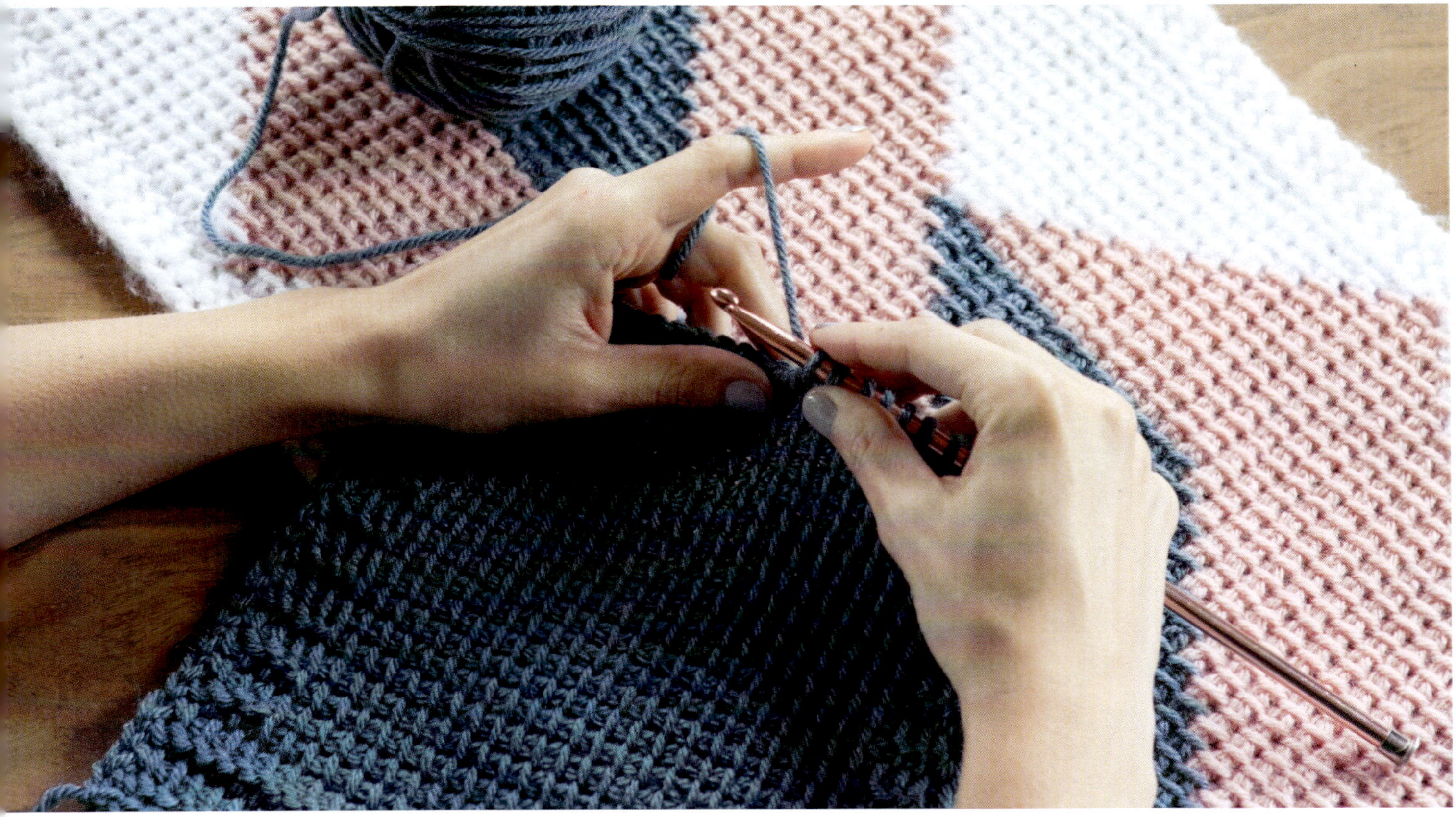

LEISURE ARTS, INC. • Maumelle, Arkansas

MARY BETH TEMPLE

Mary Beth Temple is a long time designer of knit, crochet and sewing patterns, and lover of any other type of craft that comes across her path! She can often be found crafting by the beach near her home in Wilmington, North Carolina, and makes no guarantees that there won't be sand in her samples.

With more than a dozen books to her name, Mary Beth is delighted to be back with Leisure Arts. She is also an avid teacher, especially of Tunisian crochet, and can be found teaching at conferences around the country.

You can check out her doings at www.HookedforLifePublishing.com/blog, and from there visit her various social media outlets. Mary Beth is particularly fond of making videos for her blog and her YouTube channel, www.YouTube.com/c/HookedforLifewithMaryBethTemple .

EASY

Finished Size:
60" wide x 19" deep (152.5 cm x 48.5 cm)

SHOPPING LIST

Yarn (Fine Weight) FINE 2
[5.29 ounces, 623 yards
(150 grams, 570 meters) per ball**]**:
☐ 1 ball

Tunisian Hook
☐ Size J (6 mm)
or size needed for gauge

Standard Crochet Hook
☐ Size H (5 mm) for Edging only

GAUGE INFORMATION
With Tunisian hook, in Tss,
14 sts and 16 rows = 4" (10 cm)

STITCH GUIDE
Tunisian Simple Stitch ***(Fig. 3, page 59)***
Tunisian Simple Stitch 2 Together ***(Figs. 7a & b, page 60)***

BODY
With Tunisian hook, ch 3.

Row 1 (Foundation row): Pull up a loop in second ch from hook and in last ch, return ***(Figs. 1a-c, page 59)***: 3 Tss (vertical bars).

Row 2: Skip first vertical bar, work Tss across, return.

Row 3: Ch 3, pull up a loop in second ch from hook and in next ch, work Tss under next vertical bar, work Tss2tog, return: 5 Tss.

Row 4: Skip first vertical bar, work Tss across, return.

Row 5: Ch 3, pull up a loop in second ch from hook and in next ch, work Tss across to last 2 sts, work Tss2tog, return: 7 Tss.

Repeat Rows 4 and 5 for pattern until piece measures approximately 44" (112 cm) from beginning ch; do **not** finish off.

EDGING

See Crochet Stitches, page 63.

With **right** side facing and using standard crochet hook, skip first vertical bar, inserting hook as for Tss, sc in each st across, 3 sc in point; sc in end of each row across; 3 sc in point, sc in end of next 2 rows, 5 dc in "valley" between next 2 points, ★ sc in top of next point, 5 dc in "valley" between next 2 points; repeat from ★ across, sc in end of next 2 rows, 2 sc in same st as first sc; join with slip st to first sc, finish off.

Block *(see Blocking, page 62)*.

BOOMERANG SHAWL

EASY

Finished Size:
11" wide x 65½"
circumference (28 cm x 166.5 cm)

SHOPPING LIST

Yarn (Medium Weight) 4

[4 ounces, 203 yards
(113 grams, 186 meters) per skein**]**:

- ☐ Color A (Blue) - 1 skein
- ☐ Color B (Taupe) - 1 skein
- ☐ Color C (Gold) - 1 skein

Tunisian Hook

- ☐ Size M/N (9 mm)
  or size needed for gauge

Standard Crochet Hook

- ☐ Size K (6.5 mm) for Edging only

GAUGE INFORMATION

With Tunisian hook, in Tss,
12 sts and 11 rows = 4" (10 cm)

STITCH GUIDE

Tunisian Simple Stitch ***(Fig. 3, page 59)***

COWL

BODY

First Section

With Tunisian hook and Color A, ch 30.

Row 1 (Foundation row): Pull up a loop in second ch from hook and in each ch across, return ***(Figs. 1a-c, page 59)***: 30 Tss (vertical bars).

Rows 2-30: Skip first vertical bar, work Tss across, return.

Second Section

Row 1 Forward: With Color A, skip first vertical bar, pull up a loop in each vertical bar across; drop Color A.
Row 1 Return: With Color B, YO and draw through one loop on hook, (YO and draw through 2 loops on hook) across.

Row 2 Forward: With Color B, skip first vertical bar, pull up a loop in each vertical bar across; drop Color B.
Row 2 Return: With Color A, YO and draw through one loop on hook, (YO and draw through 2 loops on hook) across.

Rows 3-29: Repeat Rows 1 and 2, 13 times; then repeat Row 1 once **more**.

Row 30 Forward: With Color B, skip first vertical bar, pull up a loop in each vertical bar across; cut Color B.
Row 30 Return: With Color A, YO and draw through one loop on hook, (YO and draw through 2 loops on hook) across changing to Color B in last st, cut Color A.

Third Section

Rows 1-30: With Color B, skip first vertical bar, work Tss across, return.

Fourth Section

Row 1 Forward: With Color B, skip first vertical bar, pull up a loop in each vertical bar across; drop Color B.
Row 1 Return: With Color C, YO and draw through one loop on hook, (YO and draw through 2 loops on hook) across.

Row 2 Forward: With Color C, skip first vertical bar, pull up a loop in each vertical bar across; drop Color C.
Row 2 Return: With Color B, YO and draw through one loop on hook, (YO and draw through 2 loops on hook) across.

Rows 3-29: Repeat Rows 1 and 2, 13 times; then repeat Row 1 once **more**.

Row 30 Forward: With Color C, skip first vertical bar, pull up a loop in each vertical bar across; cut Color C.
Row 30 Return: With Color A, YO and draw through one loop on hook, (YO and draw through 2 loops on hook) across changing to Color C in last st, cut Color B.

Fifth Section

Rows 1-30: With Color C, skip first vertical bar, work Tss across, return.

Sixth Section

Row 1 Forward: With Color C, skip first vertical bar, pull up a loop in each vertical bar across; drop Color C.
Row 1 Return: With Color A, YO and draw through one loop on hook, (YO and draw through 2 loops on hook) across.

Row 2 Forward: With Color A, skip first vertical bar, pull up a loop in each vertical bar across; drop Color A.
Row 2 Return: With Color C, YO and draw through one loop on hook, (YO and draw through 2 loops on hook) across.

Rows 3-30: Repeat Rows 1 and 2, 14 times.

Cut Color A.

Row 31: With Color C, skip first vertical bar, inserting hook as for Tss, slip st across; finish off leaving a long end for sewing.

FINISHING

With **wrong** side together, matching sts on Row 31 on Sixth Section with beginning ch, whipstitch seam ***(Fig. 13, page 62)***.

Edging

See Crochet Stitches, page 63.

Rnd 1: With **right** side facing, using standard crochet hook, and working in ends of rows, join Color A with sc in Row 1; ch 1, skip next row, ★ sc in next row, ch 1, skip next row; repeat from ★ around; join with slip st to first sc, finish off.

Rnd 2: With **right** side facing, and using standard crochet hook, join Color B with sc in any ch-1 sp; ch 1, skip next sc, ★ sc in next ch-1 sp, ch 1, skip next sc; repeat from ★ around; join with slip st to first sc, finish off.

Rnd 3: With **right** side facing, and using standard crochet hook, join Color C with sc in any ch-1 sp; ch 1, skip next sc, ★ sc in next ch-1 sp, ch 1, skip next sc; repeat from ★ around; join with slip st to first sc, finish off.

Repeat Edging across opposite edge of Body.

Block *(see Blocking, page 62)*.

EASY

Finished Size:
24" (61 cm) square
excluding edging

SHOPPING LIST

Yarn (Light Weight) 3 LIGHT

[3.5 ounces, 254 yards
(100 grams, 232 meters) per skein]:

- ☐ MC (Ecru) - 1 skein
- ☐ Color A (Red) - 1 skein
- ☐ Color B (Blue) - 1 skein
- ☐ Color C (Navy) - 1 skein
- ☐ Color D (Yellow) - 1 skein
- ☐ Color E (Gray) - 1 skein

Tunisian Hook

- ☐ Size I (5.5 mm)
  or size needed for gauge

Standard Crochet Hook

- ☐ Size H (5 mm) for edging only

Additional Supplies

- ☐ 24" (61 cm) square pillow form
- ☐ ¾ yard (.70 meters) gray brushed fleece fabric
- ☐ Sewing needle and gray thread
- ☐ Straight pins
- ☐ Large bobbins - 5

GAUGE INFORMATION

With Tunisian hook, in Tss,
12 sts and 12 rows = 4" (10 cm)

STITCH GUIDE

Tunisian Simple Stitch *(Fig. 3, page 59)*

FLOOR PILLOW

Wind MC onto bobbins.

FRONT

With Tunisian hook and MC, ch 75.

Row 1 (Foundation row): Pull up a loop in second ch from hook and in each ch across, return ***(Figs. 1a-c, page 59)***: 75 Tss (vertical bars).

Rows 2 and 3: Skip first vertical bar, work Tss across; return.

Row 4: Skip first vertical bar, work 4 Tss, with Color A work 10 Tss, with MC work 4 Tss, with Color B work 10 Tss, with MC work 4 Tss, with Color C work 10 Tss, with MC work 4 Tss, with Color D work 10 Tss, with MC work 4 Tss, with Color E work 10 Tss, with MC work 4 Tss, return ***(see Changing Colors, page 61)***.

Rows 5-66: Work in Tss, following Chart for color placement; at end of Row 66, cut all colors except MC.

KEY

- MC (Ecru)
- Color A (Red)
- Color B (Blue)
- Color C (Navy)
- Color D (Yellow)
- Color E (Gray)

CHART

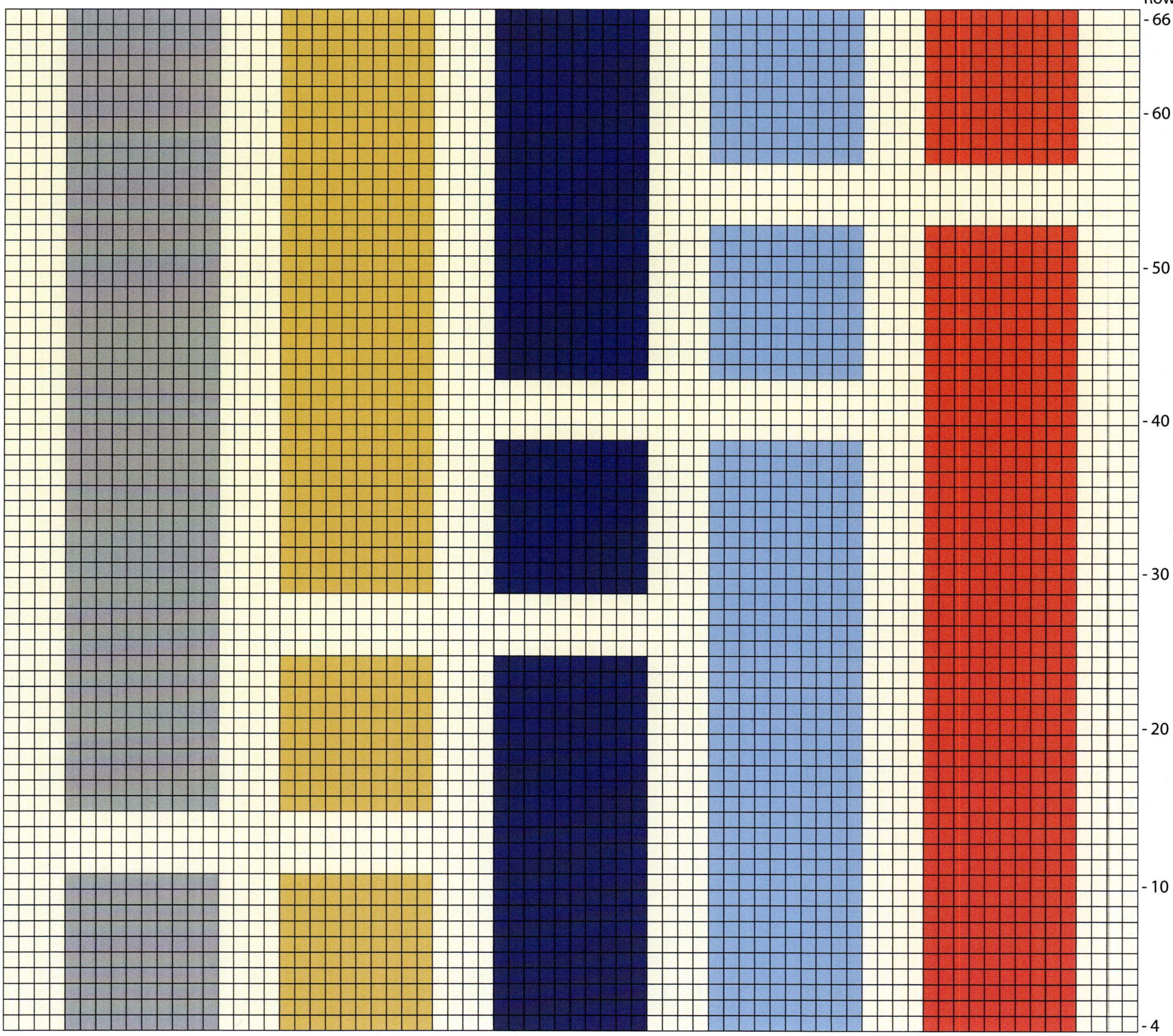

Rows 67-69: With MC, skip first vertical bar, work Tss across, return; at end of Row 69, do **not** finish off.

EDGING

See Crochet Stitches, page 63.

Slip loop onto standard crochet hook and use throughout.

Rnd 1: With MC, 2 sc in first st, inserting hook as for Tss, sc in each st across to last st, 3 sc in last st; working in ends of rows, skip first row, sc in each row across; working in free loops of beginning ch ***(Fig. 2, page 59)***, 3 sc in first ch, sc in each ch across to last ch, 3 sc in last ch; working in ends of rows, sc in each row across to last row, skip last row, sc in same st as first sc; join with slip st to first sc, finish off: 296 sc.

Rnd 2: With **right** side facing, join Color E with sc in first sc of corner 3-sc group; ch 1, 3 sc in center sc, ch 1, ★ (sc in next sc, ch 1, skip next sc) across to center sc of next corner 3-sc group, 3 sc in center sc, ch 1; repeat from ★ 2 times **more**, (sc in next sc, ch 1, skip next sc) across; join with slip st to first sc, finish off: 160 sc and 152 ch-1 sps.

Rnd 3: With **right** side facing, join MC with sc in center sc of any corner 3-sc group; 2 sc in same st, ch 1, skip next sc, ★ (sc in next ch-1 sp, ch 1, skip next sc) across to center sc of next corner 3-sc group, 3 sc in center sc, ch 1; repeat from ★ 2 times **more**, (sc in next ch-1 sp, ch 1, skip next sc) across; join with slip st to first sc, finish off: 164 sc and 156 ch-1 sps.

Rnd 4: With Color D, repeat Rnd 3: 168 sc and 160 ch-1 sps.

Rnd 5: With MC, repeat Rnd 3: 172 sc and 164 ch-1 sps.

Rnd 6: With Color C, repeat Rnd 3: 176 sc and 168 ch-1 sps.

Rnd 7: With MC, repeat Rnd 3: 180 sc and 172 ch-1 sps.

Rnd 8: With Color B, repeat Rnd 3: 184 sc and 176 ch-1 sps.

Rnd 9: With MC, repeat Rnd 3: 188 sc and 180 ch-1 sps.

Rnd 10: With Color A, repeat Rnd 3: 192 sc and 184 ch-1 sps.

Rnd 11: With MC, repeat Rnd 3; do **not** finish off: 196 sc and 188 ch-1 sps.

Rnd 12: Ch 1, sc in each sc and in each ch-1 sp around; join with slip st to first sc; finish off.

Block ***(see Blocking, page 62)***.

FINISHING

Cut fabric into a 25" (63.5 cm) square. Fold edges under ½" (12.75 mm) to wrong side and sew in place. Pin three sides of fabric to **wrong** side of Front along Rnd 1 of Edging. Sew three sides, inserting pillow form; pin remaining side, then sew closed.

EASY

Finished Size:
9¼" wide x 60" long
(from point to point)
(23.5 cm x 152.5 cm)

SHOPPING LIST

Yarn (Bulky Weight) BULKY 5

[3.5 ounces, 116 yards
(100 grams, 127 meters) per braid] and
[0.7 ounces, 23.2 yards
(20 grams, 25.4 meters) per color]:

☐ 5 braids (5 colors per braid)

Tunisian Hook

☐ Size K (6.5 mm)
or size needed for gauge

Additional Supplies

☐ Safety pins - 3

GAUGE INFORMATION

In Tss,
12 sts and 12 rows = 4" (10 cm)

STITCH GUIDE

Tunisian Simple Stitch ***(Fig. 3, page 59)***
Increase ***(Fig. 6, page 62)***
Tunisian Simple Stitch 2 Together
(Figs. 7a & b, page 60)
Tunisian Simple Stitch 3 Together ***(Fig. 8, page 60)***

HARLEQUIN SCARF

Before beginning, label the colors as Color A, Color B, Color C, Color D and Color E in any order that's pleasing to you.

BOTTOM POINT

(Make 1 each in Color A, Color B and Color C)

Leaving a 6" (15 cm) end for adding to tassel, ch 2.

Row 1 (Foundation row): Pull up a loop in second ch from hook, return ***(Figs. 1a-c, page 59)***: 2 Tss (vertical bars).

Row 2: Skip first vertical bar, increase, work Tss in last vertical bar, return: 3 Tss.

Row 3 and ALL ODD-NUMBERED ROWS: Skip first vertical bar, work Tss across, return.

Row 4: Skip first vertical bar, increase, work Tss in next vertical bar, increase, work Tss in last vertical bar, return: 5 Tss.

Row 6: Skip first vertical bar, increase, work Tss across to last vertical bar, increase, work Tss in last vertical bar, return: 7 Tss.

Rows 8-10: Repeat Rows 6 and 7 once, then repeat Row 6 once **more**: 11 Tss.

Do **not** cut yarn, place loop on hook onto safety pin to keep piece from unraveling while working remaining points; set aside.

BODY

Joining Row: Slip loop from safety pin of Color A point onto hook, skip first vertical bar, work Tss across, drop Color A, slip loop from safety pin of Color B point onto hook, skip first vertical bar, work Tss across, drop Color B, slip loop from safety pin of Color C point onto hook, skip first vertical bar, work Tss across, return working in matching colors ***(see Changing Colors, page 61)***, changing to Color D in last st, drop Color A: 33 Tss.

Rows 1-29: Continue working in Tss, following Chart Rows 1-29.

CHART

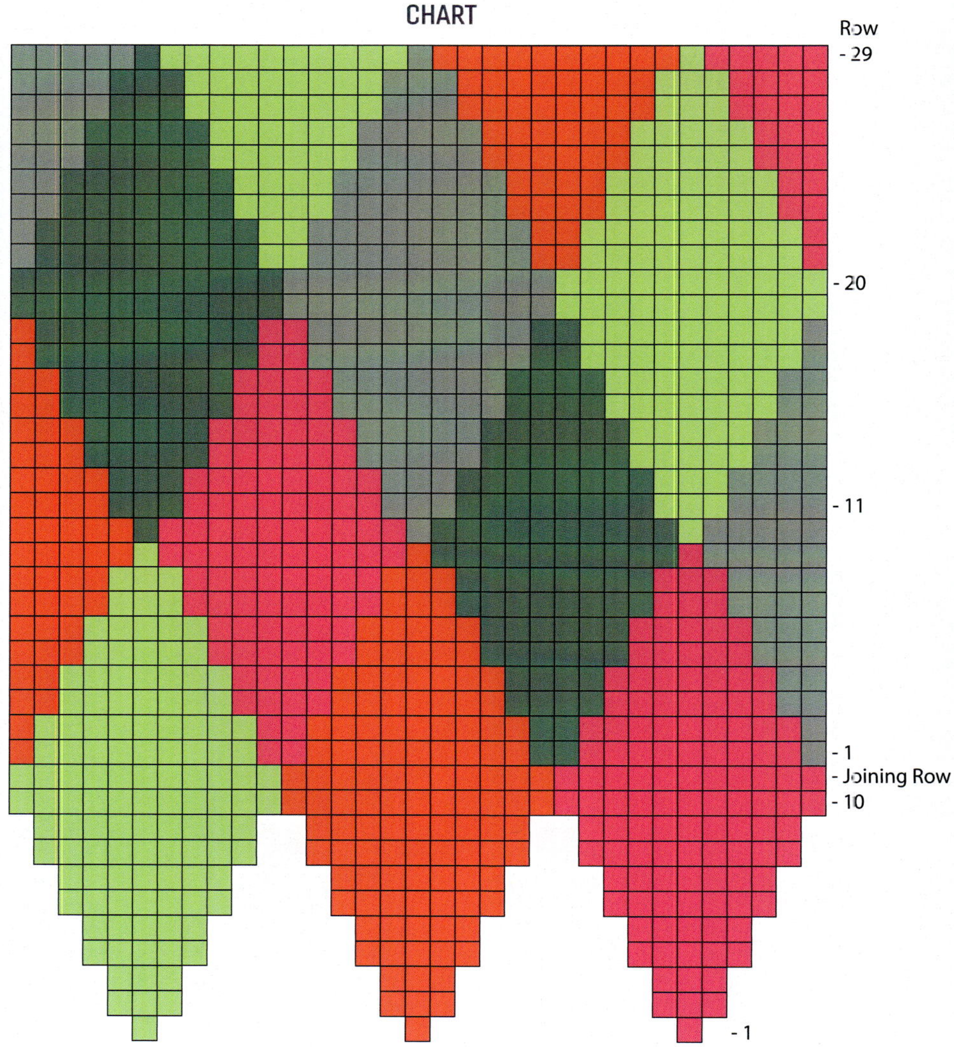

KEY

- Color A
- Color B
- Color C
- Color D
- Color E

Repeat Rows 11-29 until piece measures approximately 53" (134.5 cm) from points, ending by working Row 20; do **not** finish off the 3 Colors to be used for Top Points.

FIRST TOP POINT

Row 1: Skip first vertical bar, work Tss2tog, work 5 Tss, work Tss2tog, work Tss, leave remaining sts unworked, return: 9 Tss.

Row 2 and ALL EVEN-NUMBERED ROWS: Skip first vertical bar, work Tss across, return.

Row 3: Skip first vertical bar, work Tss2tog, work 3 Tss, work Tss2tog, work Tss, return: 7 Tss.

Row 5: Skip first vertical bar, (work Tss2tog, work Tss) twice, return: 5 Tss.

Row 7: Skip first vertical bar, work Tss3tog, work Tss, return: 3 Tss.

Row 9: Skip first vertical bar, work Tss2tog, YO and draw through both loops on hook; finish off leaving a 6" (15 cm) end.

SECOND TOP POINT

Row 1: Insert hook in first vertical bar of next diamond, YO and pull up a loop, work Tss2tog, work 5 Tss, work Tss2tog, work Tss, leave remaining sts unworked, return: 9 Tss.

Rows 2-9: Work same as First Top Point.

LAST TOP POINT

Row 1: Insert hook in first vertical bar of next diamond, YO and pull up a loop, work Tss2tog, work 5 Tss, work Tss2tog, work Tss, return: 9 Tss.

Rows 2-9: Work same as First Top Point.

FINISHING

Cut 30, 15" (38 cm) strands, 6 each of 5 colors.
Pull one strand of each color though one point. Tie group with an overhand knot to form a tassel.
Repeat for each point.
Trim ends.

Block ***(see Blocking, page 62)***.

EASY

Finished Sizes:
Hat - 20" (51 cm) head circumference
Mitts - 9" (23 cm) palm circumference

SHOPPING LIST

Yarn (Light Weight) 3

[1.75 ounces, 125 yards
(50 grams, 114 meters) per skein]:

- ☐ Color A (Gray) - 1 skein
- ☐ Color B (Ecru) - 1 skein

Tunisian Hook

- ☐ Size J (6 mm)
  or size needed for gauge

Additional Supplies

- ☐ Tapestry needle

GAUGE INFORMATION

In Tss,
14 sts and 14 rows = 4" (10 cm)

STITCH GUIDE

Tunisian Simple Stitch ***(Fig. 3, page 59)***
Increase ***(Fig. 6, page 60)***
Tunisian Simple Stitch 2 Together ***(Figs. 7a & b, page 60)***
Tunisian Crossed Stitch ***(Figs. 11a & b, page 61)***

HAT & MITT SET

CHANGING COLORS

Do **not** cut yarn unless instructed. Carry unused yarn loosely across **wrong** side ***(Fig. A)***. When working return pass, change to next color when one loop of the previous color remains on the hook ***(Fig. B)***.

When the first stitch on the next row is a different color than the last stitch on the closing, complete the last stitch with the first color of the next row.

Fig. A

Fig. B

HAT

Brim

With Color B, ch 70.

Row 1 (Foundation row): Pull up a loop in second ch from hook and in each ch across, return ***(Figs. 1a-c, page 59)***: 70 Tss (vertical bars).

Rows 2-5: Skip first vertical bar, work Tss across, return; at end of Row 5, change to Color A.

Body

Row 1: Skip first vertical bar, ★ with Color A work 2 Tss, with Color B work 2 Tss; repeat from ★ across to last st, with Color A work Tss, return.

Row 2: Skip first vertical bar, with Color A work Tss across, return.

Row 3: Skip first vertical bar, ★ with Color A work 2 Tss, with Color B work 2 Tss; repeat from ★ across to last st, with Color B work Tss, return.

Row 4: Skip first vertical bar, with Color A work 2 Tss, Tunisian Crossed St, ★ work 2 Tss, work Tunisian Crossed St; repeat from ★ across to last st, work Tss, return.

Row 5: Skip first vertical bar, with Color B work 2 Tss, ★ with Color A work 2 Tss, with Color B work 2 Tss; repeat from ★ across to last 3 sts, with Color A work Tss across, return.

Row 6: Skip first vertical bar, with Color A, ★ Tunisian Crossed St, work 2 Tss, Tunisian Crossed St; repeat from ★ across to last 3 sts, work Tss across, return.

Rows 7-13: Repeat Rows 3-6 once, then repeat Rows 3-5 once **more**.

Rows 15 and 16: Skip first vertical bar, with Color B work Tss across, return; cut Color B.

Crown

Rows 1-5: Skip first vertical bar, with Color A work Tss across, return.

Row 6: Skip first vertical bar, work 8 Tss, work Tss2tog, (work 16 Tss, work Tss2tog) 3 times, work Tss across, return: 66 Tss.

Row 7: Skip first vertical bar, (work 4 Tss, work Tss2tog) 11 times, return: 55 Tss.

Row 8: Skip first vertical bar, work Tss across, return.

Row 9: Skip first vertical bar, (work 3 Tss, work Tss2tog) 11 times, return: 44 Tss.

Row 10: Skip first vertical bar, work Tss across, return.

Row 11: Skip first vertical bar, (work 2 Tss, work Tss2tog) 11 times, return: 33 Tss.

Row 12: Skip first vertical bar, (work Tss, work Tss2tog) 11 times, return: 22 Tss.

Row 13: Skip first vertical bar, work Tss2tog across, return; finish off leaving a long end for sewing: 11 Tss.

FINISHING

Thread tapestry needle with long end, insert the needle under each vertical bar on Row 13, pull up tightly to gather top of hat; do **not** cut yarn.

Sew back seam using mattress stitch and matching colors *(Figs. 12a & b, page 62)*.

Allow bottom edge to roll forming Brim.

MITT (Make 2)

Cuff

With Color B, ch 30.

Rows 1-5: Work same as Brim: 30 Tss (vertical bars).

Body

Work same as Hat through Row 8 of Body.

Row 9: Skip first vertical bar, ★ with Color A work 2 Tss, with Color B work 2 Tss; repeat from ★ across to last st, with Color A work Tss, return.

Row 10: Skip first vertical bar, with Color B work Tss across, return; cut Color B.

Thumb Gusset

Row 1: Skip first vertical bar, with Color A work 14 Tss, increase, work Tss across, return: 31 Tss.

Row 2: Skip first vertical bar, work 14 Tss, increase, work Tss, increase, work Tss across, return: 33 Tss.

Row 3: Skip first vertical bar, work Tss across, return.

Row 4: Skip first vertical bar, work 14 Tss, increase, work 3 Tss, increase, work Tss across, return: 35 Tss.

Row 5: Skip first vertical bar, work Tss across, return.

Row 6: Skip first vertical bar, work 14 Tss, increase, work 5 Tss, increase, work Tss across, return: 37 Tss.

Palm

Row 1: Skip first vertical bar, work 14 Tss, ch 2, skip next 7 sts, work Tss across, return: 30 Tss and 2 chs.

Row 2: Skip first vertical bar, work 14 Tss, pull up a loop in each of next 2 chs, work Tss across, return: 32 Tss.

Row 3: Skip first vertical bar, work Tss across, return; finish off leaving a long end for sewing.

FINISHING

Sew side seam using mattress stitch and matching colors.

See Crochet Stitches, page 63.

Mitt trim: With Color A, inserting hook as for Tss, slip st around; join with slip st to first slip st, finish off.

Thumb trim: With Color A, inserting hook as for Tss, slip st around top edge of Thumb opening around; join with slip st to first slip st; finish off.

Allow bottom edge to roll forming Cuff.

Block *(see Blocking, page 62)*.

EASY

SHOPPING LIST

Yarn (Light Weight)

[3.5 ounces, 254 yards (100 grams, 232 meters) per skein]:

- ☐ MC (Gray) - {3-4}{4-5-5} skeins
- ☐ Color A (Blue) - 1 skein
- ☐ Color B (Yellow) - 1 skein

Tunisian Hook

- ☐ Size K (6.5 mm) **or** size needed for gauge

Standard Crochet Hook

- ☐ Size J (6 mm) for Edging only

Additional Supplies

- ☐ Large bobbins - 2
- ☐ Tapestry needle

SIZE INFORMATION

Size	Finished Chest Measurement	Length
Small	36" (91.5 cm)	25" (63.5 cm)
Medium	40" (101.5 cm)	26" (66 cm)
Large	44" (112 cm)	28" (71 cm)
X-Large	48" (122 cm)	30" (76 cm)
2X-Large	52" (132 cm)	32" (81.5 cm)

Size Note: We have printed the instructions for the sizes in different colors to make it easier for you to find:

Small in Blue
Medium in Pink
Large in Green
X-Large in Purple
2X-Large in Red
Instructions in Black apply to all sizes.

JACKET

GAUGE INFORMATION

With Tunisian hook, in Tss,
14 sts and 14 rows = 4" (10 cm)

STITCH GUIDE

Tunisian Simple Stitch ***(Fig. 3, page 59)***
Tunisian Simple Stitch 2 Together ***(Figs. 7a & b, page 60)***

Body is worked in one piece to underarm.

Wind Color A and Color B onto bobbins to be used for left front border.

BODY

With Tunisian hook and MC, ch {128-142}{156-170-184}.

Row 1 Forward (Foundation row): Pull up a loop in second ch from hook and in each ch across ***(Fig. 1a, page 59)***, drop MC.
Row 1 Return (Foundation row): With Color A, YO and draw through one loop on hook, (YO and draw through 2 loops on hook) across ***(Figs. 1b & c, page 59)***: {128-142}{156-170-184} Tss (vertical bars).

Do **not** cut yarn, carry unused yarn along **wrong** side.

Row 2 Forward: With Color B, skip first vertical bar, work Tss across; drop Color B.
Row 2 Return: With MC, YO and draw through one loop on hook, (YO and draw through 2 loops on hook) across.

Row 3 Forward: With Color A, skip first vertical bar, work Tss across; drop Color A.
Row 3 Return: With Color B, YO and draw through one loop on hook, (YO and draw through 2 loops on hook) across.

Row 4 Forward: With MC, skip first vertical bar, work Tss across; drop MC.
Row 4 Return: With Color A, YO and draw through one loop on hook, (YO and draw through 2 loops on hook) across.

Rows 5-10: Repeat Rows 2-4 twice.

Row 11 Forward: With Color B, skip first vertical bar, work 10 Tss, drop Color B; with MC, work Tss across to last 10 sts, drop MC, with second Color B, work Tss across.
Row 11 Return: With MC, YO and draw through one loop on hook, (YO and draw through 2 loops on hook) across.

Row 12 Forward: With Color A, skip first vertical bar, work 10 Tss, drop Color A; with MC, work Tss across to last 10 sts, drop MC, with second Color A, work Tss across.
Row 12 Return: With Color B, YO and draw through one loop on hook, (YO and draw through 2 loops on hook) 10 times; with MC, (YO and draw through 2 loops on hook) across to last 10 sts, with Color B, (YO and draw through 2 loops on hook) across.

Row 13 Forward: With MC, skip first vertical bar, work 10 Tss across.
Row 13 Return: With Color A, YO and draw through one loop on hook, (YO and draw through 2 loops on hook) 10 times; with MC, (YO and draw through 2 loops on hook) across to last 10 sts, with second Color A, (YO and draw through 2 loops on hook) across.

Repeat Rows 11-13 for pattern until piece measures approximately {14-15}{16-17-17}"/{35.5-38}{40.5-43-43} cm from beginning ch.

Neck Shaping

Maintaining color pattern for front borders throughout.

Rows 1 and 2: Skip first vertical bar, work 10 Tss, work Tss2tog, work Tss across to last 12 sts, work Tss2tog, work Tss across, return: {124-138}{152-166-180} Tss.

Row 3: Skip first vertical bar, work Tss across, return.

Rows 4-7: Repeat Rows 1-3 once, then repeat Row 1 once **more**: {118-132}{146-160-174} Tss.

Right Front

Row 1: Skip first vertical bar, work {28-31}{39-38-42} Tss, return; leave remaining sts unworked: {29-32}{35-39-43} Tss.

Row 2 (Decrease row): Skip first vertical bar, work 10 Tss, work Tss2tog, work Tss across to last 2 sts, work Tss2tog, return: {27-30}{33-37-41} Tss.

Row 3 (Decrease row): Skip first vertical bar, work Tss across to last 2 sts, work Tss2tog, return: {26-29}{32-36-40} Tss.

Row 4: Repeat Row 2: {24-27}{30-34-38} Tss.

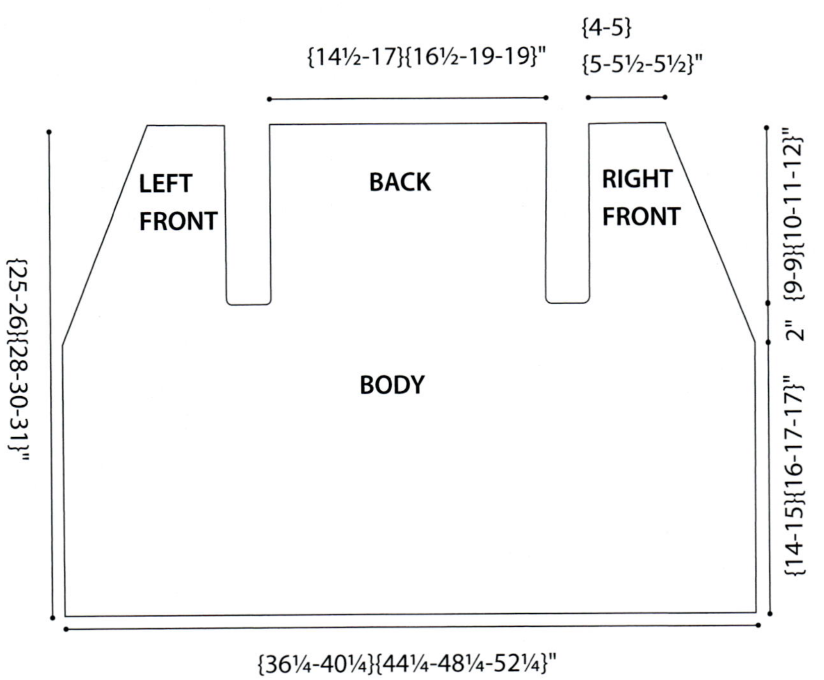

Size Large ONLY

Rows 5 and 6: Repeat Rows 3 and 4: {27} Tss.

Sizes X-Large & 2X-Large ONLY

Rows 5-7: Repeat Rows 3 and 4 once, then repeat Row 3 once **more**: {30-34} Tss.

Size 2X-Large ONLY

Rows 8-10: Repeat Rows 2 and 3 once, then repeat Row 2 once **more**: 29 Tss.

ALL SIZES

Row {5-5}{7-8-11}: Skip first vertical bar, work Tss across, return.

Row {6-6}{8-9-12} (Decrease row): Skip first vertical bar, work 10 Tss, work Tss2tog, work Tss across, return: {23-26}{26-29-28} Tss.

Rows {7-7}{9-10-13} thru {30-30}{30-32-30}: Repeat Rows {5-5}{7-8-11} and {6-6}{8-9-12}, {9-9}{9-10-9} times: {14-17}{17-19-19} Tss.

Next Row: Skip first vertical bar, work Tss across, return.

Repeat Next Row until Armhole measures approximately {9-9}{10-11-12}"/{23-23}{25.5-28-30.5} cm; finish off.

Back

Row 1: With **right** side facing and MC, beginning in first unworked vertical bar after Right Front, work {59-67}{75-81-87} Tss; leave remaining sts unworked, return: {59-67}{75-81-87} Tss.

Rows 2 thru {4-4}{4-7-10}: Work Tss2tog, work Tss across to last 2 sts, work Tss2tog, return: {51-59}{67-67-67} Tss.

Next Row: Skip first vertical bar, work Tss across, return.

Repeat Next Row until Armhole measure same as Right Front; finish off leaving a long end for sewing.

Left Front

Row 1: With **right** side facing and MC, beginning in first unworked vertical bar after Back, work Tss across, return: {29-32}{35-39-43} Tss.

Row 2 (Decrease row): Skip first vertical bar, work Tss2tog, work Tss across to within 2 sts of color change, work Tss2tog, work Tss across, return: {27-30}{33-37-41} Tss.

Row 3 (Decrease row): Skip first vertical bar, work Tss2tog, work Tss across, return: {26-29}{32-36-40} Tss.

Row 4: Repeat Row 2: {24-27}{30-34-38} Tss.

Size Large ONLY
Rows 5 and 6: Repeat Rows 3 and 4: {27} Tss.

Sizes X-Large & 2X-Large ONLY
Rows 5-7: Repeat Rows 3 and 4 once, then repeat Row 3 once **more**: {30-34} Tss.

Size 2X-Large ONLY
Rows 8-10: Repeat Rows 2 and 3 once, then repeat Row 2 once **more**: 29 Tss.

ALL SIZES
Row {5-5}{7-8-11}: Skip first vertical bar, work Tss across, return.

Row {6-6}{8-9-12} (Decrease row): Skip first vertical bar, work Tss across to within 2 sts of color change, work Tss2tog, work Tss across, return: {24-28}{33-31-27} Tss.

Rows {7-7}{9-10-13} thru {30-30}{30-32-30}: Repeat Rows {5-5}{7-8-11} and {6-6}{8-9-12}, {9-9}{9-10-9} times: {14-17}{17-19-19} Tss.

Next Row: Skip first vertical bar, work Tss across, return.

Repeat Next Row until Armhole measures same as Back; finish off leaving a long end for sewing.

Using long ends, sew shoulder seams.

SLEEVE (Make 2)

Body

With MC, ch {64-64}{71-78-85}.

Work same as Body until piece measures approximately 12" (30.5 cm) from beginning ch.

Cap Shaping

Rows 1 thru {3-3}{3-6-9}: Work Tss2tog, work Tss across to last 2 sts, work Tss2tog, return: {58-58}{65-66-67} Tss.

Finish off.

FINISHING

With **wrong** sides together and using MC, sew sleeve seams.

With MC, sew Sleeves to armhole holes.

Sleeve Edging

See Crochet Stitches, page 63.

Rnd 1: With **right** side facing and standard hook, join MC with sc at seam; sc in each st around; join with slip st to first sc.

Rnds 2 and 3: Ch 1, sc in same st as joining and in each sc around; join with slip st to first sc.

Rnd 4: Ch 1, slip st in each sc around; join with slip st to first slip st, finish off.

Body Edging

Rnd 1: With **right** side facing and standard hook, join MC with sc in st at center bottom Back edge; sc evenly around the Body, working 3 sc in each bottom corner, and decreasing 1 st at each side of back neck edge if needed to keep the edging flat; join with slip st to first sc.

Rnd 2: Ch 1, sc in same st and in each sc across to center sc of next corner 3-sc group, sc in each sc across to decrease row, 2 sc in next sc, sc in each sc to next sc2tog, sc2tog, sc in each sc across to next sc2tog, sc2tog, sc in each sc to first decrease row, 2 sc in each sc, sc in each sc across to center sc of next corner 3-sc group, 3 sc in next sc, sc in each sc across; join with slip st to first sc.

Rnd 3: Ch 1, sc in same st and in each sc across to center sc of next corner 3-sc group, sc in each sc across to center sc of next corner 3-sc group, 3 sc in each sc, sc in each sc across; join with slip st to first sc.

Rnd 4: Ch 1, slip st in each sc around; join with slip st to first st, finish off.

Block *(**see Blocking, page 62**)*.

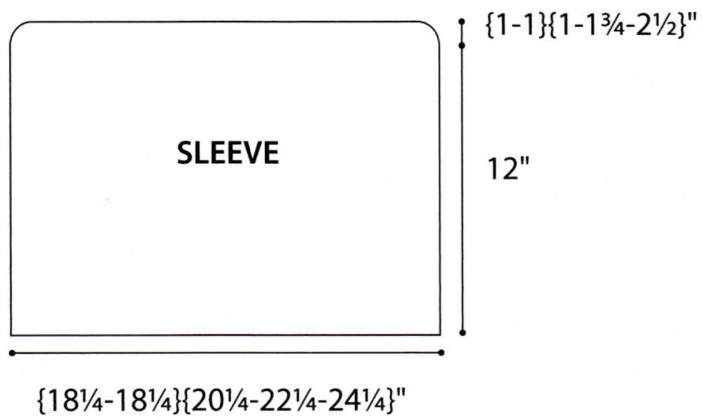

EASY

Finished Size:
35" x 51½" (89 cm x 131 cm)

SHOPPING LIST

Yarn (Medium Weight) MEDIUM 4

[5 ounces, 251 yards
(142 grams, 113 meters) per skein]:

- ☐ Blue - 3 skeins
- ☐ Pink - 2 skeins
- ☐ Purple - 2 skeins
- ☐ Gray - 2 skeins

Tunisian Crochet Hook

- ☐ Size K (6.5 mm)
  or size needed for gauge

Standard Crochet Hook

- ☐ Size J (6 mm) for edging only

Additional Supplies

- ☐ Yarn needle

GAUGE INFORMATION

Each Square = 5½" (14 cm) square

STITCH GUIDE

Tunisian Simple Stitch ***(Fig. 3, page 59)***
Tunisian Simple Stitch 3 Together ***(Fig. 7, page 60)***

MITERED SQUARES THROW

Squares are made with a join-as-you-go technique, in that you create the bottom left corner square first, then build each square onto its adjacent ones. Refer to the Placement Diagram for color and placement of Squares.

FIRST VERTICAL STRIP

First Square

With Tunisian hook and color indicated, ch 190.

Row 1 (Foundation row): Pull up a loop in horizontal bar of second ch from hook and in next 36 chs ***(Fig. 1a, page 59)***; leave remaining chs unworked, return ***(Figs. 1b & c, page 59)***: 38 Tss (vertical bars).

Row 2: Skip first vertical bar, work 17 Tss, work Tss3tog, work 17 Tss, return: 36 Tss.

Row 3: Skip first vertical bar, work 16 Tss, work Tss3tog, work 16 Tss, return: 34 Tss.

Row 4: Skip first vertical bar, work 15 Tss, work Tss3tog, work 15 Tss, return: 32 Tss.

Row 5: Skip first vertical bar, work 14 Tss, work Tss3tog, work 14 Tss, return: 30 Tss.

Row 6: Skip first vertical bar, work 13 Tss, work Tss3tog, work 13 Tss, return: 28 Tss.

Row 7: Skip first vertical bar, work 12 Tss, work Tss3tog, work 12 Tss, return: 26 Tss.

Row 8: Skip first vertical bar, work 11 Tss, work Tss3tog, work Tss, return: 24 Tss.

Row 9: Skip first vertical bar, work 10 Tss, work Tss3tog, work 10 Tss, return: 22 Tss.

Row 10: Skip first vertical bar, work 9 Tss, work Tss3tog, work 9 Tss, return: 20 Tss.

Row 11: Skip first vertical bar, work 8 Tss, work Tss3tog, work 8 Tss, return: 18 Tss.

Row 12: Skip first vertical bar, work 7 Tss, work Tss3tog, work 7 Tss, return: 16 Tss.

Row 13: Skip first vertical bar, work 6 Tss, work Tss3tog, work 6 Tss, return: 14 Tss.

Row 14: Skip first vertical bar, work 5 Tss, work Tss3tog, work 5 Tss, return: 12 Tss.

Row 15: Skip first vertical bar, work 4 Tss, work Tss3tog, work 4 Tss, return: 10 Tss.

Row 16: Skip first vertical bar, work 3 Tss, work Tss3tog, work 3 Tss, return: 8 sts.

Row 17: Skip first vertical bar, work 2 Tss, work Tss3tog, work 2 Tss, return: 6 Tss.

Row 18: Skip first vertical bar, work Tss, work Tss3tog, work Tss, return: 4 Tss.

Row 19: Skip first vertical bar, work Tss3tog; finish off.

PLACEMENT DIAGRAM

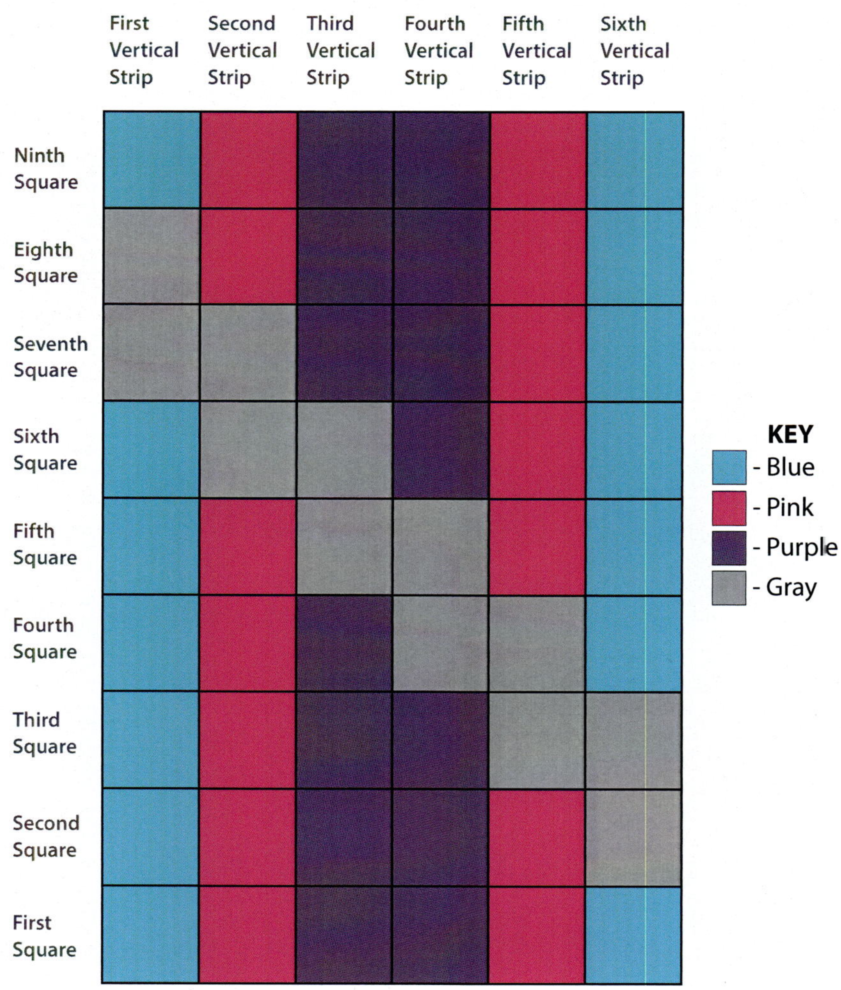

Second Square

Row 1 (Foundation row): With next color indicated, work Tss in next 19 rows across top edge of the previous square, pull up a loop in next 19 chs of foundation ch, leave remaining chs unworked, return: 38 Tss.

Beginning with Row 2, complete same as First Square.

Third through Eighth Squares

Repeat Second Square.

Ninth Square

Row 1 (Foundation row): With next color indicated, work Tss in next 19 rows across top edge of the Eighth Square, pull up a loop in last 19 chs of foundation ch, return: 38 Tss.

Beginning with Row 2, complete same as First Square.

SECOND VERTICAL STRIP

See Crochet Stitches, page 63.

First Square

With **right** side facing, join next color indicated with slip st to bottom right corner of First Square of previous strip; ch 19.

Row 1 (Foundation row): Pull up a loop in second ch from hook and in each ch across, work Tss in next 19 rows along side of same square, return: 38 Tss.

Beginning with Row 2 of First Square of First Vertical Strip, complete same as First Square.

Second Square

Foundation row: With next color indicated, work Tss in next 19 rows across top edge of the previous square and in next 19 rows along side of next square, return: 38 Tss.

Beginning with Row 2 of Second Square of First Vertical Strip, complete same as Second Square.

Third through Ninth Squares

Repeat Second Square.

THIRD THROUGH SIXTH VERTICAL STRIPS

Repeat Second Vertical Strip.

EDGING

Rnd 1: With **right** side facing and standard crochet hook, join Blue with sc in any corner; sc in each st around, working 3 sc in each corner; join with slip st in first sc.

Rnd 2: Ch 3 **(counts as first dc)**, dc in next sc and in each sc around, working 5 dc in center sc of each 3-sc corner; join with slip st to first dc.

Rnd 3: Ch 1, sc in each dc around, working 3 sc in center dc of each 5-dc corner; join with slip st in first sc, finish off.

Block ***(see Blocking, page 62)***.

EASY

Finished Size:
11½" x 18½" (29 cm x 47 cm)

SHOPPING LIST

Yarn (Medium Weight) MEDIUM 4

[4 ounces, 200 yards
(113 grams, 184 meters) per skein]:
- ☐ MC (Gray or White) - 1 skein
- ☐ Color A (Orange) - 1 skein
- ☐ Color B (Blue) - 1 skein
- ☐ Color C (White or Gray) - 1 skein

Tunisian Crochet Hook

- ☐ Size I (5.5 mm) **or** size needed for gauge

Standard Crochet Hook

- ☐ Size H (5 mm) for edging only

Additional Supplies

- ☐ Large bobbins - 7

GAUGE INFORMATION

With Tunisian hook, in Tss
14 sts and 14 rows = 4" (10 cm)

STITCH GUIDE

Tunisian Simple Stitch *(Fig. 3, page 59)*

Wind 2 bobbins each of Color A and Color B and one bobbin of Color C.

BODY

With Tunisian hook and MC, ch 10 changing to Color A in last ch, ch 15 changing to MC in last ch ***(see Changing Colors, page 61)***, ch 39: 64 chs.

Row 1 (Foundation row): With MC work 38 Tss, with Color A work 7 Tss, with Color C work Tss, with Color A work 7 Tss, with MC work Tss across, return: 64 Tss (vertical bars).

Rows 2-41: Working in Tss, follow Chart Rows 2-33 once, then follow Charts Rows 12-19 once **more** for accent column; at end of Row 41, do **not** finish off MC, do **not** cut Colors A and C and cut Color B.

EDGING

See Crochet Stitches, page 63.

Slip loop onto standard crochet hook, 3 sc in first st, inserting hook as for Tss, sc in next 39 sts changing to Color C in last sc, cut MC, sc in next 4 sts changing to Color A in last sc, cut Color C, sc in next 7 sts changing to Color C in last sc, cut Color A, sc in next 4 sts changing to MC in last sc, cut Color C, sc in next 9 sts, 3 sc in last st; sc in end of each row across; working in free loops of beginning ch ***(Fig. 2, page 59)***, 3 sc in first ch, sc in next 9 chs changing to Color A in last sc, cut MC, sc in next 15 chs changing to MC in last sc, cut Color A, sc in each ch across to last ch, 3 sc in last ch; sc in end of each row across; join with slip st to first sc, finish off.

Block ***(see Blocking, page 62)***.

PLACEMAT

CHART

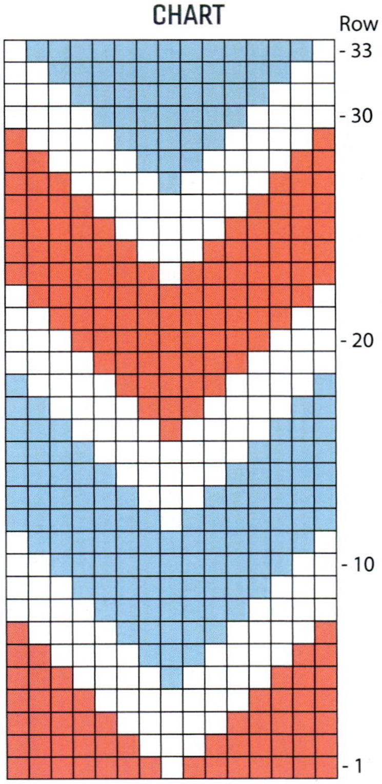

KEY

- Color A (Orange)
- Color B (Blue)
- Color C (White)

CHART

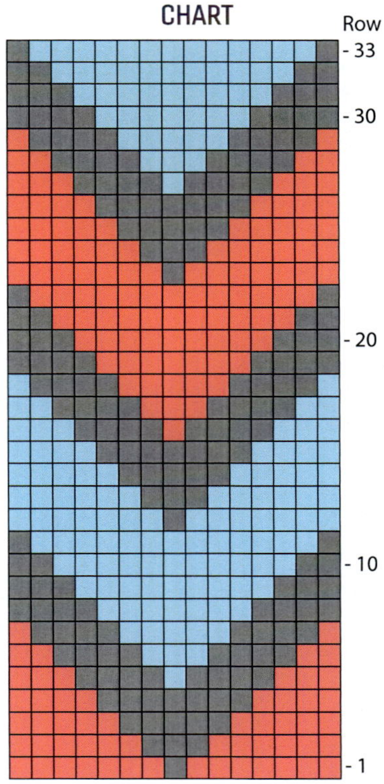

KEY

- Color A (Orange)
- Color B (Blue)
- Color C (Gray)

EASY

Finished Size:
27" (68.5 cm) long (neckline to tip)

SHOPPING LIST

Yarn (Light Weight) LIGHT 3

[5.3 ounces, 590 yards
(150 grams, 540 meters) per skein**]**:

- ☐ 3 skeins

Tunisian Hook

- ☐ Size I (5.5 mm)
  or size needed for gauge

Standard Crochet Hook

- ☐ Size I (5.5 mm) for edging only

Additional Supplies

- ☐ Tapestry needle
- ☐ Large bobbins - 2

GAUGE INFORMATION

With Tunisian hook, in Tss,
14 sts and 14 rows = 4" (10 cm)

STITCH GUIDE

Tunisian Simple Stitch *(Fig. 3, page 59)*

PONCHO

The color pattern is random and comes from the color changes in the yarn EXCEPT for the "arrow" sections which are stitched in. To get the most contrast, I started each section in a different place in the color sequence, and for the small sections near the arrow which need a bobbin, I wound yarn from the outside of the 2 skeins onto 2 bobbins, one to be used on each Panel.

RECTANGLE (Make 2)

With Tunisian hook and first skein, ch 61.

Row 1: Pull up a loop in second ch from hook and in next 20 chs, with second skein pull up a loop in next 20 chs, with third skein pull up a loop in each ch across, return ***(Figs. 1a-c, page 59 and Changing Colors, page 61)***: 61 Tss (vertical bars).

Rows 1-7: Skip first vertical bar, work 20 Tss, with second skein work 20 Tss, with third skein work 20 Tss, return.

Row 8: Skip first vertical bar, work 20 Tss, with second skein work 20 Tss, with third skein work 20 Tss, changing to bobbin color, return.

Row 9: Skip first vertical bar, with bobbin work Tss, with first skein work 20 Tss, with second skein work 20 Tss, with third skein work 19 Tss, return.

Row 10: Skip first vertical bar, with bobbin work 2 Tss, with first skein work 20 Tss, with second skein work 20 Tss, with third skein work 18 Tss, return.

Row 11: Skip first vertical bar, with bobbin work 3 Tss, with first skein work 20 Tss, with second skein work 20 Tss, with third skein work 17 Tss, return.

Row 12: Skip first vertical bar, with bobbin work 4 Tss, with first skein work 20 Tss, with second skein work 20 Tss, with third skein work 16 Tss, return.

Row 13: Skip first vertical bar, with bobbin work 5 Tss, with first skein work 20 Tss, with second skein work 20 Tss, with third skein work 15 Tss, return.

Row 14: Skip first vertical bar, with bobbin work 6 Tss, with first skein work 20 Tss, with second skein work 20 Tss, with third skein work 14 Tss, return.

Row 15: Skip first vertical bar, with bobbin work 7 Tss, with first skein work 20 Tss, with second skein work 20 Tss, with third skein work 13 Tss, return.

Row 16: Skip first vertical bar, with bobbin work 8 Tss, with first skein work 20 Tss, with second skein work 20 Tss, with third skein work 12 Tss, return.

Row 17: Skip first vertical bar, with bobbin work 9 Tss, with first skein work 20 Tss, with second skein work 20 Tss, with third skein work 11 Tss, return.

Row 18: Skip first vertical bar, with bobbin work 10 Tss, with first skein work 20 Tss, with second skein work 20 Tss, with third skein work 10 Tss, return.

Row 19: Skip first vertical bar, with bobbin work 11 Tss, with first skein work 20 Tss, with second skein work 20 Tss, with third skein work 9 Tss, return.

Row 20: Skip first vertical bar, with bobbin work 12 Tss, with first skein work 20 Tss, with second skein work 20 Tss, with third skein work 8 Tss, return.

Row 21: Skip first vertical bar, with bobbin work 13 Tss, with first skein work 20 Tss, with second skein work 20 Tss, with third skein work 7 Tss, return.

Row 22: Skip first vertical bar, with bobbin work 14 Tss, with first skein work 20 Tss, with second skein work 20 Tss, with third skein work 6 Tss, return.

Row 23: Skip first vertical bar, with bobbin work 15 Tss, with first skein work 20 Tss, with second skein work 20 Tss, with third skein work 5 Tss, return.

Row 24: Skip first vertical bar, with bobbin work 16 Tss, with first skein work 20 Tss, with second skein work 20 Tss, with third skein work 4 Tss, return.

Row 25: Skip first vertical bar, with bobbin work 17 Tss, with first skein work 20 Tss, with second skein work 20 Tss, with third skein work 3 Tss, return.

Row 26: Skip first vertical bar, with bobbin work 18 Tss, with first skein work 20 Tss, with second skein work 20 Tss, with third skein work 2 Tss, return.

Row 27: Skip first vertical bar, with bobbin work 19 Tss, with first skein work 20 Tss, with second skein work 20 Tss, with third skein work Tss, return.

Rows 28: Skip first vertical bar, with bobbin work 20 Tss, with first skein work 20 Tss, with second skein work 20 Tss, return.

Row 29: Skip first vertical bar, with bobbin work 19 Tss, with first skein work 20 Tss, with second skein work 20 Tss, with third skein work Tss, return.

Row 30: Skip first vertical bar, with bobbin work 18 Tss, with first skein work 20 Tss, with second skein work 20 Tss, with third skein work 2 Tss, return.

Row 31: Skip first vertical bar, with bobbin work 17 Tss, with first skein work 20 Tss, with second skein work 20 Tss, with third skein work 3 Tss, return.

Row 32: Skip first vertical bar, with bobbin work 16 Tss, with first skein work 20 Tss, with second skein work 20 Tss, with third skein work 4 Tss, return.

Row 33: Skip first vertical bar, with bobbin work 15 Tss, with first skein work 20 Tss, with second skein work 20 Tss, with third skein work 5 Tss, return.

Row 34: Skip first vertical bar, with bobbin work 14 Tss, with first skein work 20 Tss, with second skein work 20 Tss, with third skein work 6 Tss, return.

Row 35: Skip first vertical bar, with bobbin work 13 Tss, with first skein work 20 Tss, with second skein work 20 Tss, with third skein work 7 Tss, return.

Row 36: Skip first vertical bar, with bobbin work 12 Tss, with first skein work 20 Tss, with second skein work 20 Tss, with third skein work 8 Tss, return.

Row 37: Skip first vertical bar, with bobbin work 11 Tss, with first skein work 20 Tss, with second skein work 20 Tss, with third skein work 9 Tss, return.

Row 38: Skip first vertical bar, with bobbin work 10 Tss, with first skein work 20 Tss, with second skein work 20 Tss, with third skein work 10 Tss, return.

Row 39: Skip first vertical bar, with bobbin work 9 Tss, with first skein work 20 Tss, with second skein work 20 Tss, with third skein work 11 Tss, return.

Row 40: Skip first vertical bar, with bobbin work 8 Tss, with first skein work 20 Tss, with second skein work 20 Tss, with third skein work 12 Tss, return.

Row 41: Skip first vertical bar, with bobbin work 7 Tss, with first skein work 20 Tss, with second skein work 20 Tss, with third skein work 13 Tss, return.

Row 42: Skip first vertical bar, with bobbin work 6 Tss, with first skein work 20 Tss, with second skein work 20 Tss, with third skein work 14 Tss, return.

Row 43: Skip first vertical bar, with bobbin work 5 Tss, with first skein work 20 Tss, with second skein work 20 Tss, with third skein work 15 Tss, return.

Row 44: Skip first vertical bar, with bobbin work 4 Tss, with first skein work 20 Tss, with second skein work 20 Tss, with third skein work 16 Tss, return.

Row 45: Skip first vertical bar, with bobbin work 3 Tss, with first skein work 20 Tss, with second skein work 20 Tss, with third skein work 17 Tss, return.

Row 46: Skip first vertical bar, with bobbin work 2 Tss, with first skein work 20 Tss, with second skein work 20 Tss, with third skein work 18 Tss, return.

Row 47: Skip first vertical bar, with bobbin work Tss, with first skein work 20 Tss, with second skein 20 Tss, with third skein work 19 Tss, return.

Row 48: Skip first vertical bar, with first skein work 20 Tss, with second skein work 20 Tss, with third skein work 20 Tss, return.

Repeat Row 48 for pattern until piece measures approximately 31" (78.5 cm) from beginning ch; finish off.

FINISHING

With **right** sides facing and using diagram as a guide, sew rectangles together.

Diagram

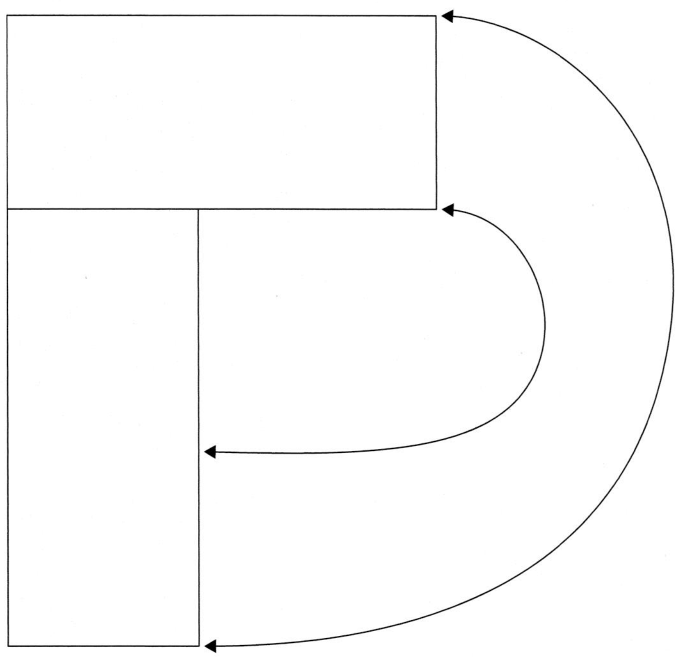

Body Edging

See Crochet Stitches, page 63.

Rnd 1: With standard crochet hook, join yarn with sc in either point; sc in same st, sc in each st and in each row across to next point, 3 sc in point, sc in each st and in each row around, sc in same st as first sc; join with slip st to first sc.

Rnd 2: Ch 1, 3 sc in same st as joining, sc in each sc across to center sc of next 3-sc group, 3 sc in center sc, sc in each sc around; join with slip st to first sc.

Rnd 3: Ch 1, do **not** turn; working from **left** to **right**, work reverse sc in each sc around ***(Figs. 14a-d, page 62)***; join with slip st to first st, finish off.

Neck Edging

Rnd 1: With standard crochet hook, join yarn with sc in any st; ★ sc in each st and in each row across to within one row of seam, [pull up a loop in next row, skip seam, pull up a loop in next row, YO and draw through all 3 loops on hook **(counts as one sc)**], place marker in sc just made; repeat from ★ once **more**, sc in each st and in each row around; join with slip st to first sc.

Rnd 2: Ch 1, sc in each sc across to marked sc, remove marker, sc2tog, sc in each sc across to next marked sc, remove marker, sc2tog, sc in each sc around; join with slip st to first sc.

Rnd 3: Ch 1, do **not** turn; working from **left** to **right**, work reverse sc in each sc around; join with slip st to first st, finish off.

Block ***(see Blocking, page 62)***.

EASY

Finished Size:
16" (40.5 cm) square

SHOPPING LIST

Yarn (Medium Weight) MEDIUM 4

[3.5 ounces, 270 yards
(100 grams, 247 meters) per skein]:
- ☐ 3 skeins

Tunisian Hook
- ☐ Size I (5.5 mm)
  or size needed for gauge

Standard Crochet Hook
- ☐ Size H (5 mm) for edging only

Additional Supplies
- ☐ Tapestry needle
- ☐ 16" (40.5 cm) square pillow form

GAUGE INFORMATION

With Tunisian hook, in Tss,
13 sts and 13 rows = 4" (10 cm)

STITCH GUIDE

Tunisian Simple Stitch ***(Fig. 3, page 59)***
Increase ***(Fig. 6, page 60)***
Tunisian Simple Stitch 2 Together
(Figs. 7a & b, page 60)

FRONT

Increase Section

With Tunisian hook, ch 3.

Foundation row (Right side): Pull up a loop in second ch from hook and in last ch, return ***(Figs. 1a-c, page 59)***: 3 Tss (vertical bars).

Row 2: Skip first vertical bar, (increase, work Tss) twice, return: 5 Tss.

Row 3: Increase, work Tss across to last st, increase, work Tss, return: 7 Tss.

Repeat Row 3 for pattern until side edges measure approximately 16" (40.5 cm).

Decrease Section

Row 1: Skip first vertical bar, Tss2tog, work Tss across to last 2 sts, work Tss2tog, return.

Repeat Row 1 for pattern until 3 sts remain.

Last Row: Pull up a loop under next vertical bar and under last vertical bar, YO and draw through 3 loops on hook; finish off.

BACK

I began two skeins of yarn at the same time, in the same place in the color sequence, and alternated one row per skein to make the color blocks wider.

Work same as Front using two skeins as instructed.

FINISHING

See Crochet Stitches, page 63.

With **wrong** sides together and standard crochet hook, join yarn with sc in any st; sc in each st or row around, working 3 sc in each corner, and inserting pillow form before closing; join with slip st to first sc, finish off.

Block *(**see Blocking, page 62**)*.

THROW PILLOW

EASY

Finished Size:
14" square x 11" tall
(35.5 cm x 28 cm)

SHOPPING LIST

Yarn (Bulky Weight) 5

[3.5 ounces, 120 yards
(100 grams, 109 meters) per skein]:
- ☐ MC (Green) - 3 skeins
- ☐ Color A (Pink) - 1 skein
- ☐ Color B (White) - 1 skein

Tunisian Hook

- ☐ Size N/P (10 mm)
  or size needed for gauge

Standard Crochet Hook

- ☐ Size M/N (9 mm) for edging

Additional Supplies

- ☐ Yarn needle
- ☐ 14" (35.5 cm) square piece of plastic canvas
- ☐ Chenille stems - 24

GAUGE INFORMATION

With Tunisian hook, in Tks,
8 sts and 11 rows = 4" (10 cm)

STITCH GUIDE

Tunisian Simple Stitch ***(Fig. 3, page 59)***
Tunisian Knit Stitch ***(Fig. 4, page 59)***

BODY

With Tunisian hook and MC, ch 29.

Foundation row (Right side): Pull up a loop in horizontal bar of second ch from hook and in each ch across ***(Fig. 1a, page 59)***, return ***(Figs. 1b & c, page 59)***: 29 Tss (vertical bars).

Row 2: Skip first vertical bar, work Tss across, return.

Row 3: Skip first vertical bar, work Tks across, return.

Repeat Row 3 for pattern until piece measures approximately 36" (91.5 cm) from beginning ch; finish off.

SIDE (Make 2)

With Tunisian hook, MC, and beginning at bottom edge, ch 29.

Foundation row (Right side): Pull up a loop in horizontal bar of second ch from hook and in each ch across, return changing to Color A in last st ***(see Changing Colors, page 61)***: 29 Tss (vertical bars).

Rows 2 and 3: Skip first vertical bar, work Tks across, return.

Row 4: Skip first vertical bar, with Color A, work Tks across to last st, work Tss, return changing to Color B in last st.

STORAGE BASKET

Rows 5 and 6: Skip first vertical bar, work Tks across to last st, work Tss, return.

Row 7 (Decrease row): Skip first vertical bar, work Tks2tog, work Tks across to last 3 sts, work Tks2tog, work Tss, return changing to Color A in last st: 27 sts.

Rows 8-19: Repeat Rows 2-7 twice: 23 sts.

Rows 20 and 21: Skip first vertical bar, work Tks across to last st, work Tss, return.

Row 22: Skip first vertical bar, work Tks across to last st, work Tss, return changing to MC in last st.

Row 23: Skip first vertical bar, work Tss across, return; finish off.

FINISHING

See Crochet Stitches, page 63.

Joining Row: With **wrong** sides of Body and Side together, working through **both** layers, and using standard crochet hook, join MC with sc in end of first row; sc in end of each row across; matching ends of rows on Body and beginning ch of Side, sc in each st across; sc in end of each row across; finish off.

Repeat with remaining Side.

Top Edging

Rnd 1: With standard crochet hook, inserting hook as for Tss, join MC with sc in sc at seam; sc in each st around; join with slip st to first sc.

Rnd 2: Ch 1, sc in same st as joining and in each st around; join with slip st to first sc.

Rnd 3: Ch 1, do **not** turn; working from **left** to **right**, work reverse sc in each sc around ***(Figs. 14a-d, page 62)***; join with slip st to first st, finish off.

Corner Support (Make 4)

Using 2 stems for 3 sections, braid stems. Using yarn needle and MC, sew one Corner Support to each corner seam along inside of basket; folding excess down so it doesn't show.

Insert plastic canvas into bottom of Basket. With MC and yarn needle, tack plastic canvas into place at corners.

Block ***(see Blocking, page 62)***.

EASY

Finished Size:
10" square x 12" high
(25 cm x 30.5 cm)

SHOPPING LIST

Yarn (Medium Weight)

MEDIUM 4

[2.8 ounces, 138 yards
(80 grams, 126 meters) per skein**]**:

- ☐ Color A (Teal) - 4 skeins
- ☐ Color B (Light Teal) - 4 skeins

Tunisian Hook

- ☐ Size I (5.5 mm)
  or size needed for gauge

Standard Crochet Hook

- ☐ Size I (5.5 mm) for Sides only

Additional Supplies

- ☐ Tapestry needle
- ☐ Large bobbin

GAUGE INFORMATION

With Tunisian hook, in Tss,
16 sts and 16 rows = 4" (10 cm)

STITCH GUIDE

Tunisian Simple Stitch ***(Fig. 3, page 59)***

TOTE

Wind Color A onto bobbin.

BASE

With Tunisian hook and Color A, ch 20; finish off. Set aside to be used on Center.

First End

With Color A, ch 41.

Row 1 (Foundation row): Pull up a loop in second ch from hook and in each ch across, return *(**Figs. 1a-c, page 59**)*: 41 Tss (vertical bars).

Rows 2-5: Skip first vertical bar, work Tss across to last st, work Tss, return.

Rows 6-15: Skip first vertical bar, work 10 Tss, with Color B work 20 Tss, with second Color A, work Tss across, return.

Cut unused yarn.

Rows 16-20: Skip first vertical bar, with Color A work Tss across, return.

Center

Row 1: Ch 20, pull up a loop in second ch from hook and in each ch across (**Second End**), pull up a loop in first vertical of First End, with Color B work 40 Tss across, with second Color A, pull up a loop in each ch across ch-20 set aside (**Third End**), return: 81 Tss (vertical bars).

Rows 2-10: Skip first vertical bar, work 20 Tss, with Color B work 40 Tss, with Color A work 20 Tss, return.

Rows 11-30: Skip first vertical bar, work 5 Tss, with first Color B work 10 Tss, with next Color A work 5 Tss, with next Color B work 10 Tss, with next Color A work 20 Tss, with next Color B work 10 Tss, with next Color A work 5 Tss, with next Color B work 10 Tss, with next Color A work 5 Tss, return.

Rows 31-40: Skip first vertical bar, work 20 Tss, with Color B work 40 Tss, with Color A work 20 Tss, return.

Fourth End

See Crochet Stitches, page 63.

Row 1: Skip first vertical bar, with Color A inserting hook as for Tss, slip st in next 20 sts, work 40 Tss, leave remaining sts unworked, return: 41 Tss (vertical bars).

Rows 2-20: Work same as First End.

Finish off.

FINISHING

With **right** sides of First and Second Ends together and working in ends of rows through **both** layers, join Color A with slip st in first row; slip st in each row across.
Repeat for remaining three corners.

Upper Mesh

Rnd 1: With standard crochet hook, inserting hook as for Tss and working in ends of rows, join Color B with sc in any seam; sc in each st around; join with slip st to first sc: 160 sc.

Rnd 2: Ch 4 **(counts as first dc plus ch 1, now and throughout)**, skip next sc, ★ dc in next sc, ch 1, skip next sc; repeat from ★ around; join with slip st to first dc: 80 dc.

Rnds 3-10: Ch 4, (dc in next dc, ch 1) around; join with slip st to first dc.

Rnd 11: Ch 1, sc in each dc and in each ch-1 sp around; join with slip st to first dc, finish off: 160 sc.

First Top Border

Row 1: With Color A, working in both loops, pull up a loop in first sc and in next 19 sc, leave remaining sc unworked, return: 20 Tss (vertical bars).

Row 2: With Color B, work Tss across, return; finish off.

Row 3: With Color A, work Tss across, return, finish off.

Second & Third Top Border

Row 1: With Color A, working in both loops, pull up a loop in next unworked sc and in next 19 sc, leave remaining sc unworked, return: 20 Tss.

Complete same as First Top Border.

Fourth Top Border

Row 1: With Color A, working in both loops, pull up a loop in next unworked sc and in last 19 sc, return: 20 Tss (vertical bars).

Complete same as First Top Border.

With Color A, sew Top Borders together in each corner.

Trim: With standard crochet hook and inserting hook as for Tss, join Color A in with sc in any st on Row 3 of Top Border; sc in each st around; join with slip st to first sc, finish off.

HANDLE (Make 2)

With Color A, ch 7.

Row 1 (Foundation row): Pull up a loop in second ch from hook and in each ch across, return: 7 Tss (vertical bars).

Row 2: Skip first vertical bar, work Tss across, return.

Repeat Row 2 until piece measures approximately 22" (56 cm) from beginning ch.

Last Row: Skip first vertical bar, inserting hook as for Tss, slip st across; finish off.

With Color A, sew one Handle securely to **right** side of any corner, sew remaining end to opposite corner.
Sew last Handle to remaining two corners in same manner.

Block ***(see Blocking, page 62)***.

EASY

Finished Size:
8½" wide x 11" high
(21.5 cm x 28 cm) excluding fringe

SHOPPING LIST

Yarn (Light Weight) LIGHT 3

[5 ounces, 362 yards
(140 grams, 362 meters) per skein]:

- ☐ MC (White) - 1 skein
- ☐ Color A (Green) - 1 skein
- ☐ Color B (Red) - 1 skein
- ☐ Color C (Mint) - 1 skein
- ☐ Color D (Gray) - 1 skein
- ☐ Color E (Peach) - 1 skein
- ☐ Color F (Tan) - 1 skein

Tunisian Hook

- ☐ Size I (5.5 mm)
  or size needed for gauge

Standard Crochet Hook

- ☐ Smaller size hook to attach fringe

Additional Supplies

- ☐ Large bobbin
- ☐ Round wooden dowel - 3/8" diameter x 12" long (1 cm x 30.5 cm)
- ☐ Tapestry needle
- ☐ Glue - optional

GAUGE INFORMATION

With Tunisian hook, in Tss
16 sts and 16 rows = 4" (10 cm)

STITCH GUIDE

Tunisian Simple Stitch *(Fig. 3, page 59)*

WALL HANGING

Wind MC onto bobbin.

BODY

With Tunisian hook and MC, ch 36.

Row 1 (Foundation row): Pull up a loop in second ch from hook and in each ch across, return ***(Figs. 1a-c, page 59)***: 36 Tss (vertical bars).

Rows 2-5: Skip first vertical bar, work Tss across, return.

Row 6: Skip first vertical bar, work 9 Tss, with Color A work Tss, with Color B work 15 Tss, with Color C work Tss, with bobbin MC work Tss across, return.

Rows 7-33: Continue working in Tss following chart.

Cut bobbin MC.

Rows 34-43: Skip first vertical bar, work Tss across, return.

Finish off leaving a long end for sewing.

FINISHING

Casing

Fold top edge to **wrong** side; sew Row 43 along Row 33 to form casing.

Fringe

Cut 5 strands of each color, each 15" (38 cm) long.
Fold one strand in half.
With **wrong** side facing and using a crochet hook, draw the folded end up through first stitch and pull the loose ends through the folded end ***(Fig. A)***; draw the knot up **tightly** ***(Fig. B)***. Repeat, in each st across in desired color order.

CHART

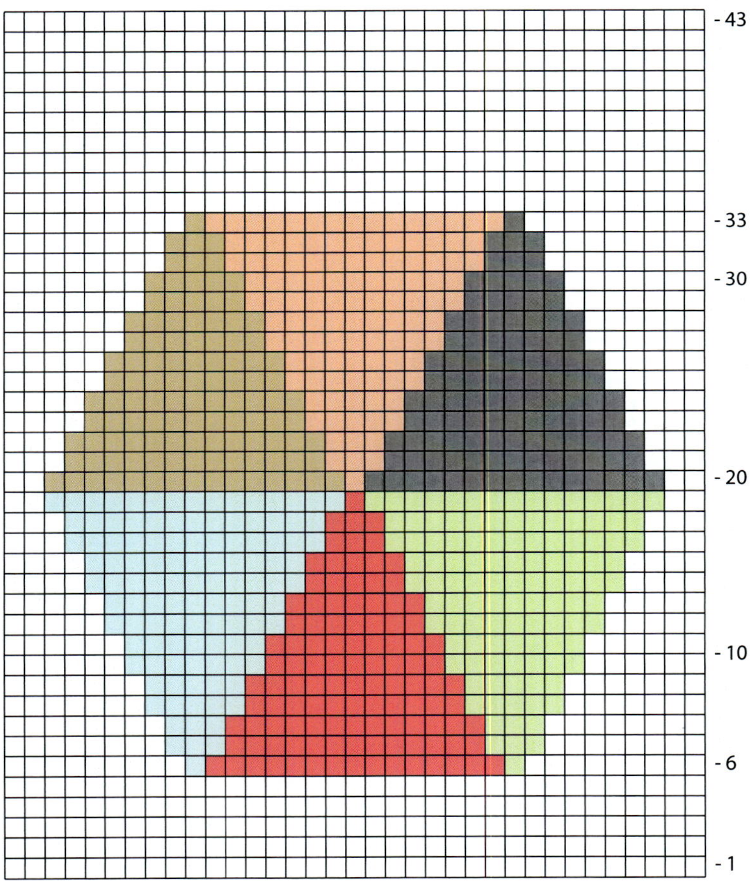

KEY

- □ - MC (White)
- ■ - Color A (Green)
- ■ - Color B (Red)
- ■ - Color C (Mint)
- ■ - Color D (Gray)
- ■ - Color E (Peach)
- ■ - Color F (Tan)

Fig. A

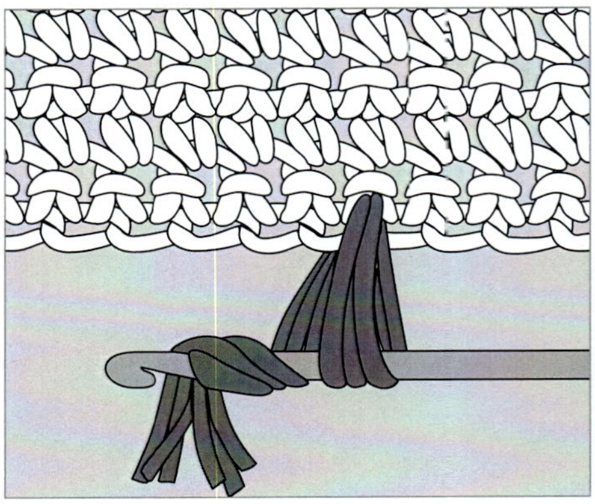

Fig. B

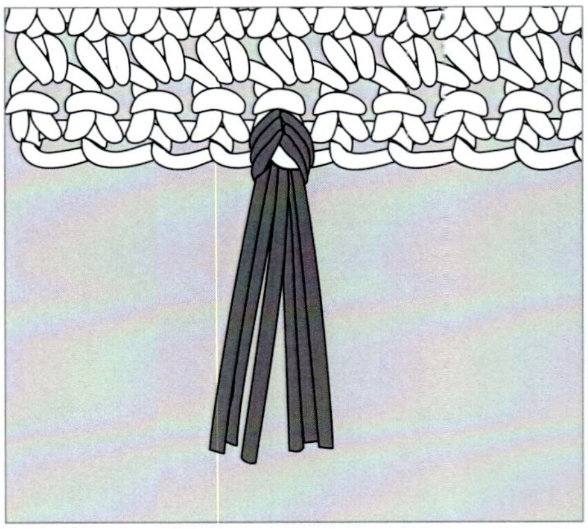

Tie groups of 7 strands together in an overhand knot to form tassels.
Lay flat on a hard surface and trim the ends.

Hanging Cord

Cut 14 50" (127 cm) strands of yarn, two of each color.
Holding 7 colors together, fasten one end to a stationary object **or** have another person hold it; twist until **tight**.
Fold in half and let it twist on itself.

Repeat for remaining strands.

Tie cut edges of both cords together approximately 1" (2.5 cm) from end to form center top fringe.

Insert dowel into casing; then place folded end of each cord on each end of dowel.
Glue to dowel if desired.

Block ***(see Blocking, page 62)***.

EASY

Finished Size:
12" wide x 56" long
(30.5 cm x 142 cm)

SHOPPING LIST

Yarn (Medium Weight) MEDIUM 4

[3.5 ounces, 170 yards
(100 grams, 156 meters) per skein]:

- ☐ MC (White) - 2 skeins
- ☐ Color A (Pink) -2 skeins
- ☐ Color B (Teal) - 1 skein

Tunisian Hook

- ☐ Size K (6.5 mm)
  or size needed for gauge

Additional Supplies

- ☐ Large bobbins - 3

GAUGE INFORMATION

In Tss,
14 sts and 12 rows = 4 " (10 cm)

STITCH GUIDE

Tunisian Simple Stitch *(Fig. 3, page 59)*
Tunisian Purl Stitch *(Fig. 5, page 59)*

TABLE RUNNER

Wind Color B onto one bobbin and Color A onto two bobbins.

BOTTOM BORDER

With MC, ch 46.

Foundation row (Right side): Pull up a loop in horizontal bar of second ch from hook and in each ch across ***(Fig. 1a, page 59)***, return ***(Figs. 1b & c, page 59)***: 29 Tss (vertical bars).

Rows 1-3: Skip first vertical bar, work Tps across, return.

BODY

Row 1: Skip first vertical bar, work 3 Tps (border), work 13 Tss, with Color A work 12 Tss, with Color B work Tss, with second MC work 13 Tss, work 3 Tps (border), return ***(see Changing Colors, page 61)***.

Chart does not show the side borders of Tps.

Rows 2-156: Follow Chart Rows 2-26; then follow Chart Rows 1-26, 5 times; at end of Row 156, do **not** finish off MC; cut Color A and Color B.

TOP BORDER

Rows 1-3: Skip first vertical bar, work Tps across, return.

Row 4: Skip first vertical bar, work Tss across, return.

Row 5: Skip first vertical bar, inserting hook as for Tss, slip st across; finish off.

Block ***(see Blocking, page 62)***.

CHART

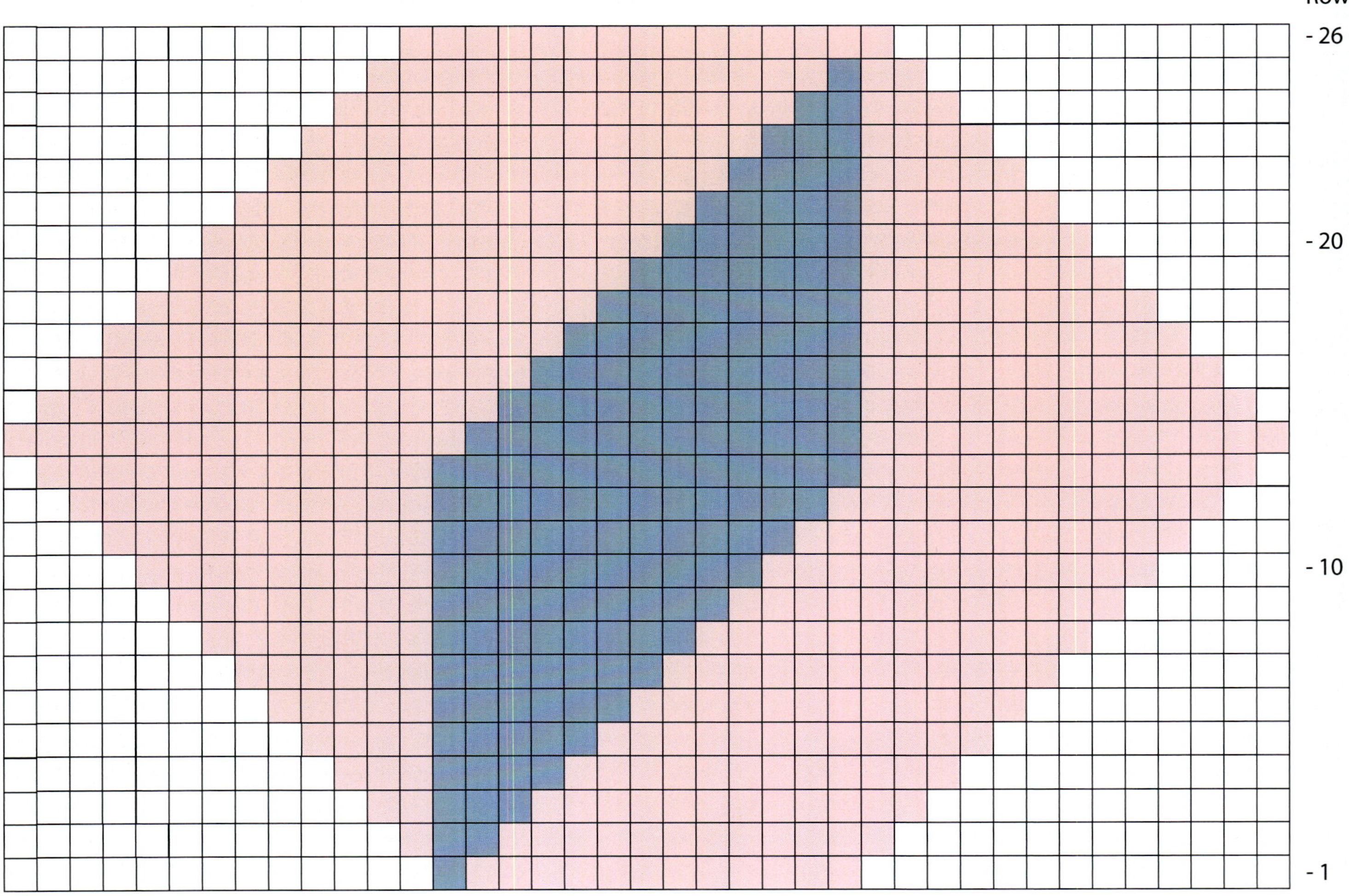

KEY

- MC (White)
- Color A (Pink)
- Color B (Teal)

GENERAL INSTRUCTIONS

ABBREVIATIONS

ch(s)	chain(s)
cm	centimeters
dc	double crochet(s)
MC	Main Color
mm	millimeters
Rnd(s)	Round(s)
sc	single crochet(s)
sp(s)	space(s)
st(s)	stitch(es)
tog	together
Tks	Tunisian Knit Stitch
Tks2tog	Tunisian Knit Stitch 2 Together
Tps	Tunisian Purl Stitch
Tss	Tunisian Simple Stitch
Tss2tog	Tunisian Simple Stitch 2 Together
Tss3tog	Tunisian Simple Stitch 3 Together
YO	yarn over

CROCHET TERMINOLOGY		
UNITED STATES		INTERNATIONAL
slip stitch (slip st)	=	single crochet (sc)
single crochet (sc)	=	double crochet (dc)
half double crochet (hdc)	=	half treble crochet (htr)
double crochet (dc)	=	treble crochet (tr)
treble crochet (tr)	=	double treble crochet (dtr)
double treble crochet (dtr)	=	triple treble crochet (ttr)
triple treble crochet (tr tr)	=	quadruple treble crochet (qtr)
skip	=	miss

SYMBOLS & TERMS

★ — work instructions following ★ as many **more** times as indicated in addition to the first time.

( ) or [ ] — work enclosed instructions **as many** times as specified by the number immediately following **or** contains explanatory remarks.

colon (:) — the number(s) given after a colon at the end of a row or round denote(s) the number of stitches and spaces you should have on that row or round.

GAUGE

Exact gauge is **essential** for proper size or fit. Before beginning your project, make a sample swatch in the yarn and hook specified. After completing the swatch, measure it, counting your stitches and rows carefully. If your swatch is larger or smaller than specified, **make another, changing hook size to get the correct gauge.** Keep trying until you find the size hook that will give you the specified gauge.

Yarn Weight Symbol & Names	LACE 0	SUPER FINE 1	FINE 2	LIGHT 3	MEDIUM 4	BULKY 5	SUPER BULKY 6	JUMBO 7
Type of Yarns in Category	Fingering, size 10 crochet thread	Sock, Fingering, Baby	Sport, Baby	DK, Light Worsted	Worsted, Afghan, Aran	Chunky, Craft, Rug	Super Bulky, Roving	Jumbo, Roving
Crochet Gauge* Ranges in Single Crochet to 4" (10 cm)	32-42 sts**	21-32 sts	16-20 sts	12-17 sts	11-14 sts	8-11 sts	6-9 sts	5 sts and fewer
Advised Hook Size Range	Steel*** 6 to 8, Regular hook B-1	B-1 to E-4	E-4 to 7	7 to I-9	I-9 to K-10½	K-10½ to M/N-13	M/N-13 to Q	Q and larger

*GUIDELINES ONLY: The chart above reflects the most commonly used gauges and hook sizes for specific yarn categories.

** Lace weight yarns are usually crocheted with larger hooks to create lacy openwork patterns. Accordingly, a gauge range is difficult to determine. Always follow the gauge stated in your pattern.

*** Steel crochet hooks are sized differently from regular hooks–the higher the number, the smaller the hook, which is the reverse of regular hook sizing.

■□□□ **BASIC**	Projects using basic stitches. May include basic increases and decreases.
■■□□ **EASY**	Projects may include simple stitch patterns, color work, and/or shaping.
■■■□ **INTERMEDIATE**	Projects may include involved stitch patterns, color work, and/or shaping.
■■■■ **COMPLEX**	Projects may include complex stitch patterns, color work, and/or shaping using a variety of techniques and stitches simultaneously.

CROCHET HOOKS

U.S.	B-1	C-2	D-3	E-4	F-5	G-6	7	H-8	I-9	J-10	K-10½	L-11	M/N-13	N/P-15	P/Q	Q	S
Metric - mm	2.25	2.75	3.25	3.5	3.75	4	4.5	5	5.5	6	6.5	8	9	10	15	16	19

FOUNDATION ROW

Chain the number indicated in the pattern.

Forward Pass: Pull up a loop in horizontal bar of second ch from hook and each ch across ***(Fig. 1a)***.

Return Pass: YO and draw through one loop on hook ***(Fig. 1b)***, (YO and draw through 2 loops on hook) across ***(Fig. 1c)***: one loop.

Fig. 1a

Fig. 1b

Fig. 1c

FREE LOOPS OF BEGINNING CHAIN

Work into loop(s) indicated ***(Fig. 2)***.

Fig. 2

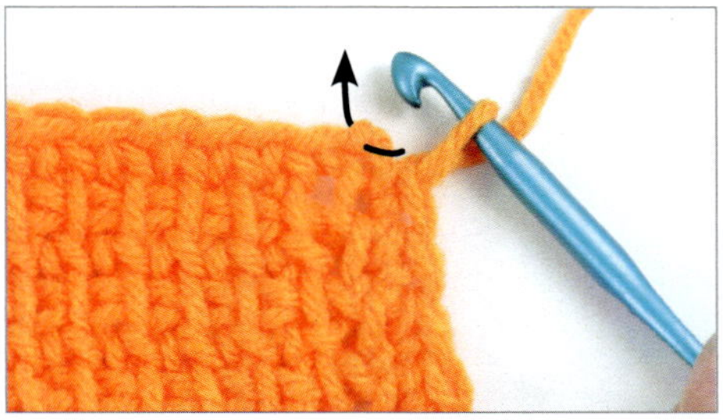

TUNISIAN SIMPLE STITCH

(abbreviated Tss)

Insert hook from **right** to **left** under next vertical bar ***(Fig. 3)***, YO and pull up a loop.

Fig. 3

TUNISIAN KNIT STITCH

(abbreviated Tks)

Insert hook from **front** to **back** between front and back vertical bars of next st ***(Fig. 3)***, YO and pull up a loop.

Fig. 4

TUNISIAN PURL STITCH

(abbreviated Tps)

With yarn in **front** of work, insert hook from **right** to **left** under next vertical bar ***(Fig. 4)***, YO and pull up a loop.

Fig. 5

INCREASE

Insert hook in ch **before** next vertical bar ***(Fig. 6)***, YO and pull up a loop.

Fig. 6

TUNISIAN SIMPLE STITCH 2 TOGETHER

(abbreviated Tss2tog)

Insert hook from **right** to **left** under next 2 vertical bars ***(Fig. 7a)***, YO and draw through 2 loops on hook ***(Fig. 7b)***.

Fig. 7a

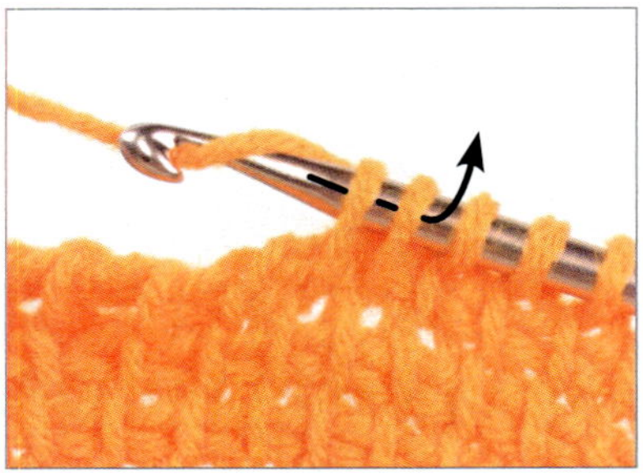

Fig. 7b

TUNISIAN SIMPLE STITCH 3 TOGETHER

(abbreviated Tss3tog)

Insert hook from **right** to **left** under next 3 vertical bars ***(Fig. 8)***, YO and draw through 3 loops on hook.

Fig. 8

TUNISIAN KNIT 2 TOGETHER

(abbreviated Tks2tog)

Insert hook from **front** to **back** between the **front** and **back** vertical bars of the next 2 stitches ***(Fig. 9)***. YO and pull loop through the 2 vertical bars.

Fig. 9

CHANGING COLORS

End of Return Pass

Work across to last 2 loops on hook. Drop the old yarn and with the new yarn ***(Fig. 10a)***, yarn over and draw through both loops on hook.

Fig. 10a

In Middle of a Row on Return Pass

Drop the old yarn and with the new yarn, yarn over and draw through 2 loops on hook ***(Fig. 10b)***.

Fig. 10b

TUNISIAN CROSSED STITCH

(uses 2 sts)

Skip next vertical bar, insert hook from **right** to **left** under next vertical bar ***(Fig. 11a)***, YO and pull up a loop, insert hook from **right** to **left** under skipped vertical bar, YO and pull up a loop ***(Fig. 11b)***.

Fig. 11a

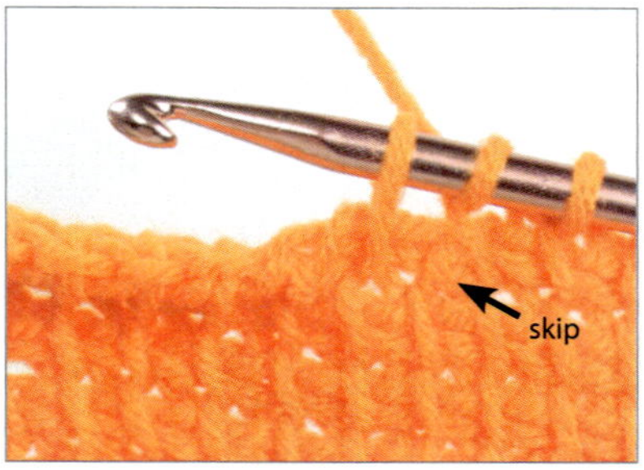

Fig. 11b

MATTRESS STITCH

With **right** side of both edges facing you and matching rows, sew through both sides once to secure the seam. Insert the needle from **back** to **front** through two strands on one side ***(Fig. 12a)***, then from **back** to **front** on the other side ***(Fig. 12b)***. Continue in this manner drawing the seam together as you work. This will create a flat seam.

Fig. 12a

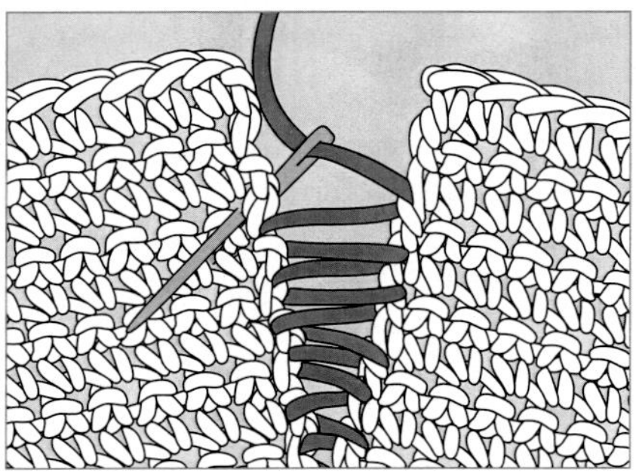

Fig. 12b

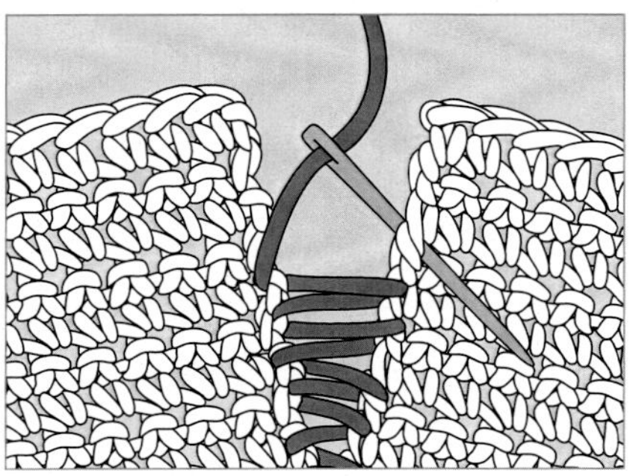

WHIPSTITCH

With **right** side together, sew through stitches on both sides once to secure the beginning of the seam. Insert the needle from **front** to **back** through both loops on both sides ***(Fig. 13)***. Bring the needle around and insert it from **front** to **back** through next loops of both sides. Continue in this manner across, keeping the sewing yarn fairly loose.

Fig. 13

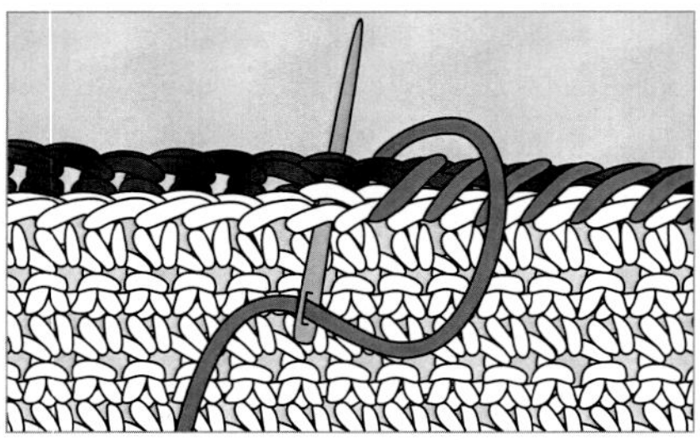

BLOCKING

Follow instructions on yarn label or block as follows:
Submerge piece in cool water. Roll piece in a clean terry towel and gently press out the excess moisture. Lay piece flat and allow to dry completely, away from heat and sunlight.

REVERSE SINGLE CROCHET

(abbreviated reverse sc)

Working from left to right, ★ insert hook in st to right of hook ***(Fig. 14a)***, YO and draw through, under and to left of loop on hook (2 loops on hook) ***(Fig. 14b)***, YO and draw through both loops on hook ***(Fig. 14c)*** (**reverse sc made, *Fig. 14d)***; repeat from ★ around.

Fig. 14a

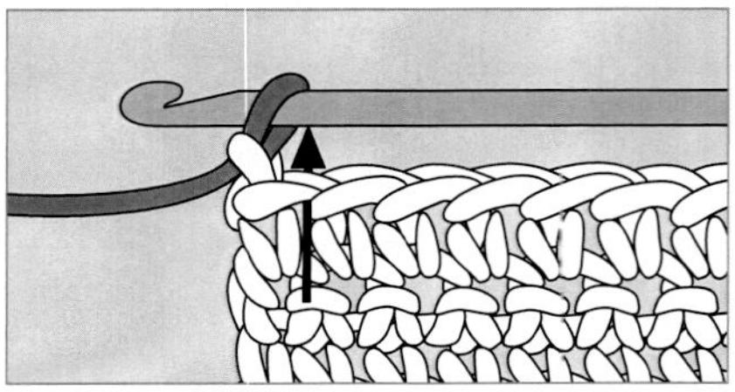

Fig. 14b

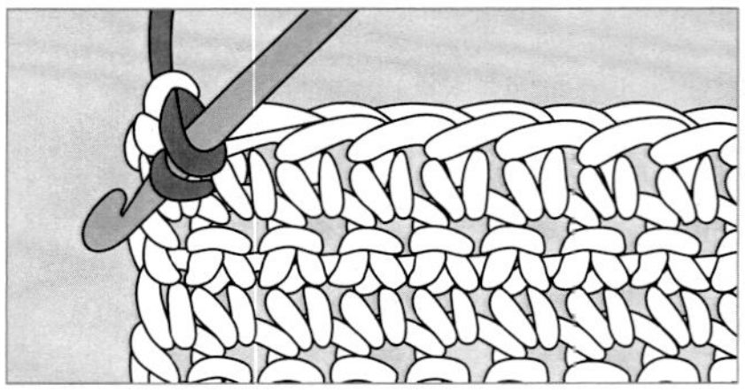

Fig. 14c

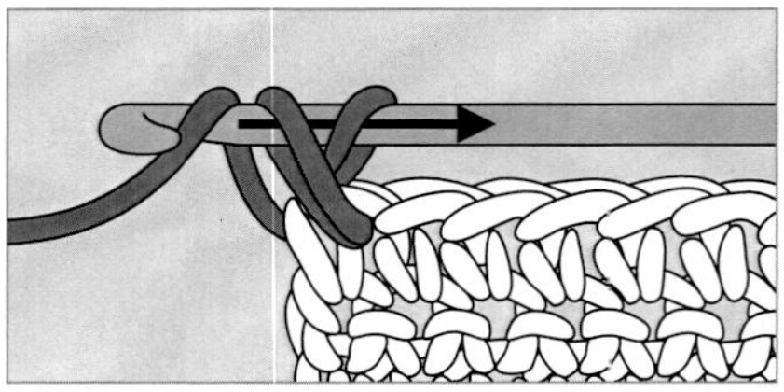

Fig. 14d

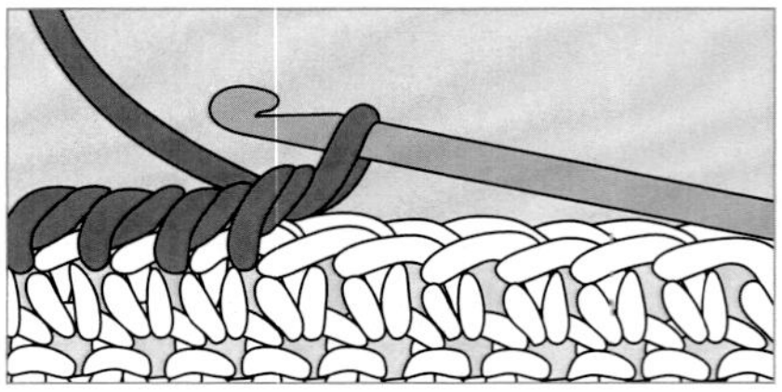

CROCHET STITCHES

Single Crochet *(abbreviated sc)*

Insert hook in stitch indicated, YO and pull up a loop, YO and draw through both loops on hook *(Fig. 15)*.

Fig. 15

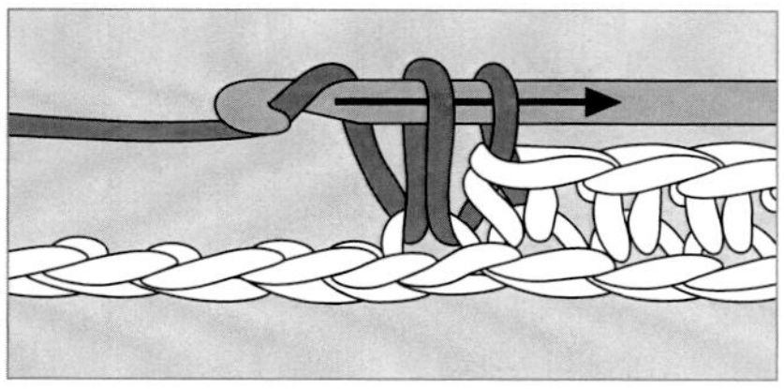

Double Crochet *(abbreviated dc)*

YO, insert hook in stitch indicated, YO and pull up a loop (3 loops on hook), YO and draw through 2 loops on hook ***(Fig. 16a)***, YO and draw through remaining 2 loops on hook ***(Fig. 16b)***.

Fig. 16a

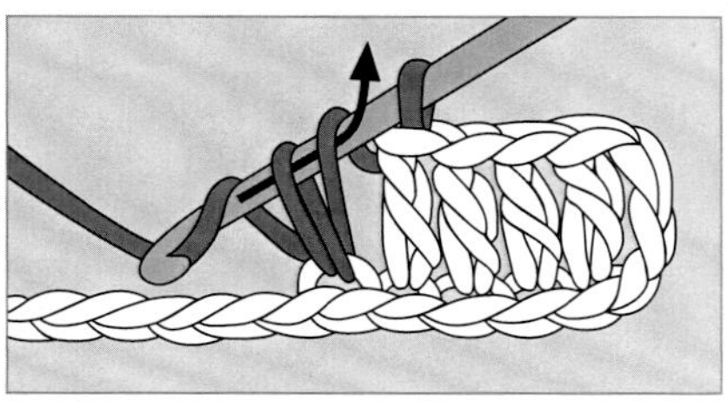

Fig. 16b

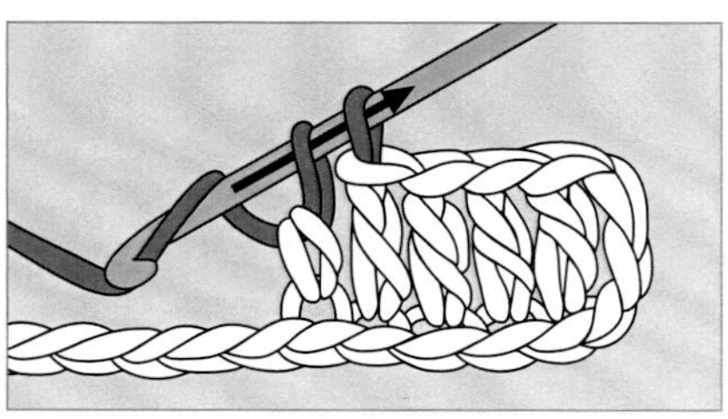

Joining With Sc

When instructed to join with sc, begin with a slip knot on hook. Insert hook in stitch indicated, YO and draw through both loops on hook ***(Figs. 17a & b)***.

Fig. 17a

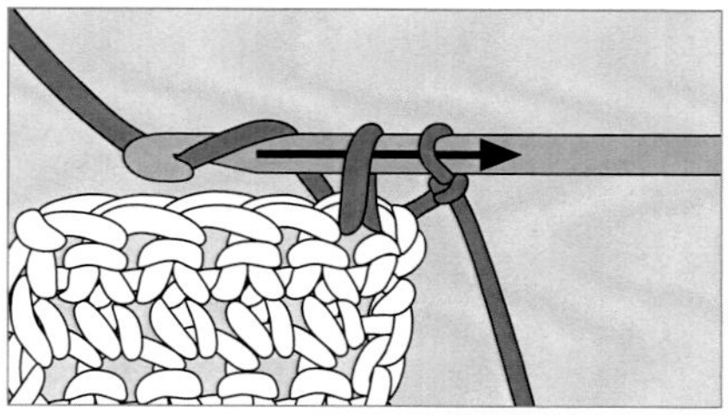

Fig. 17b

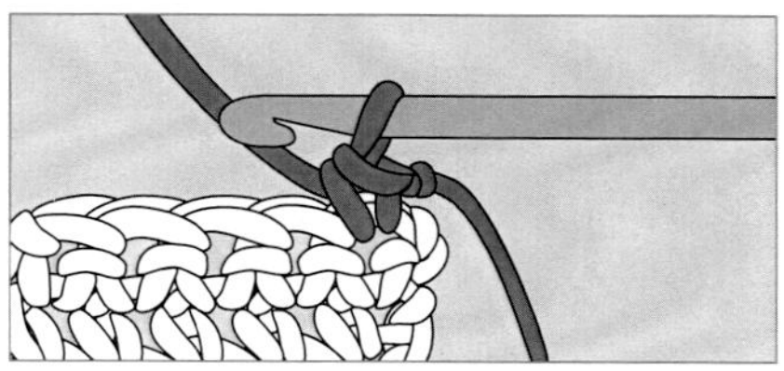

Single Crochet 2 Together

Pull up a loop in each of next 2 sts, YO and draw through all 3 loops on hook ***(Figs. 18a & b)*** **(counts as one sc)**.

Fig. 18a

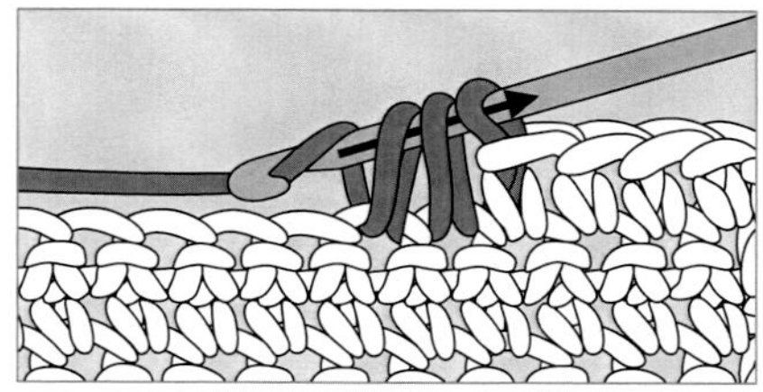

Fig. 18b

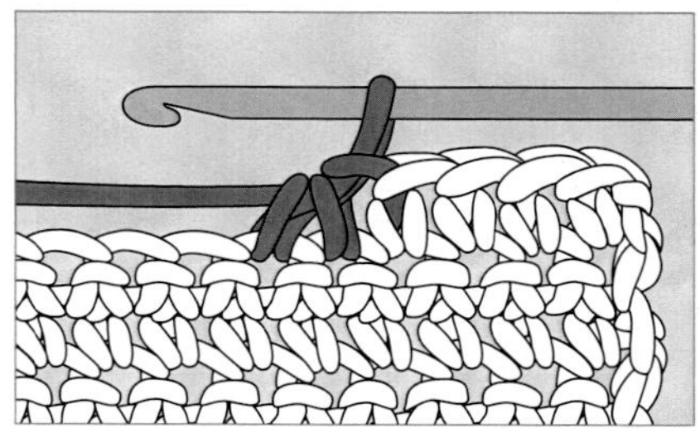

YARN INFORMATION

The items in this book were made using a variety of yarns. Any brand of the specific weight of yarn may be used. It is best to refer to the yardage/meters when determining how many balls or skeins to purchase. Remember, to achieve the same look, it is the weight of yarn that is important, not the brand of yarn.

For your convenience, listed below are the specific yarns used to create our photography models. Because yarn manufacturers make frequent changes to their product lines, you may sometimes find it necessary to use a substitute yarn or to search for the discontinued product at alternate suppliers (locally or online).

BOOMERANG SHAWL
Red Heart® It's A Wrap Rainbow™
#9368 Seaglass

COWL
Premier Everyday®
Color A (Blue) - #18 Cornflower
Color B (Taupe) - #52 Chinchilla
Color C (Gold) - #28 Mustard

FLOOR PILLOW
Lion Brand® Vanna's Style
MC (Ecru) - #098 Ecru
Color A (Gray) - #149 Silver
Color B (Yellow) - #159 Mustard
Color C (Navy) - #110 Navy
Color D (Blue) - #107 Sky
Color E (Red) - #134 Tomato

HARLEQUIN SCARF
Caron® X Pantone™
#01020 Fuchsia Foliage

HAT & MITT SET
Patons® Classic Wool DK Superwash™
MC (Ecru) - #12008 Aran
CC (Gray) - # 12042 Dark Gray Heather

JACKET
Lion Brand® Vanna's Style
MC (Gray) - #149 Silver
Color A (Yellow) - #159 Mustard
Color B (Blue) - #107 Sky

MITERED SQUARE THROW
Lion Brand® Heartland®
Blue - #178 Pinnacles
Pink - #195 Biscayne
Purple - #147 Hot Springs
Gray - #150 Mount Rainier

PLACEMAT
Lily® Sugar 'n Cream®
Gray - #01042 Overcast
White - #00001 White
Orange - #01699 Tangerine
Blue - #01712 Hot Blue

PONCHO
Lion Brand® Mandala®
#210 Pegasus

THROW PILLOW
Red Heart® Unforgettable™
#3962 Sugarcane

STORAGE BASKET
Bernat® Roving™
Green - #00014 Lichin
Pink - #00717 Quartz Pink
White - #00100 Rice Paper

TOTE
Bernat® Handicrafter®
Light Teal - #01245 Robins Egg
Teal - #01745 Teal

WALL HANGING
Bernat® Softee® Baby™
MC (White) - #2000 White
Color A (Green) - #30221 Soft Fern
Color B (Red) - #30424 Soft Red
Color C (Mint) - #02004 Mint
Color D (Gray) - #30044 Flannel
Color E (Peach) - #30410 Soft Peach
Color F (Tan) - #30010 Little Mouse

TABLE RUNNER
Lion Brand® Vanna's Choice®
White - #100 White
Teal - #108 Dusty Blue
Pink - #101 Pink

Library of Congress Control Number: 2019933137

We have made every effort to ensure that these instructions are accurate and complete. We cannot, however, be responsible for human error, typographical mistakes, or variations in individual work.

Production Team: Instructional/Technical Editor - Lois J. Long; Senior Graphic Artist - Lora Puls; Photo Stylist - Lori Wenger; and Photographer - Jason Masters. Mitered Squares Throw made and instructions tested by Kay Shultz.

Made in U.S.A.